SCHOLASTIC

Grammar Games & Activities
That Boost Writing Skills

by Immacula A. Rhodes

3 0614 00307 4152

OCT 13 2016

SOUTH COUNTRY LIBRARY

NEW YORK • TORONTO • LONDON • AUCKLAND • SYDNEY
MEXICO CITY • NEW DELHI • HONG KONG • BUENOS AIRES

Teaching *Resources*

To Diane and Mary,
for helping me grow in understanding of the language of life.

"God has given us eternal life, and this life is in his Son."—1 John 5:11

Scholastic Inc. grants teachers permission to photocopy the pattern pages from this book for classroom use. No other part of this publication may be reproduced in whole or in part, or stored in a retrieval system, or transmitted in any form or by any means, electronic, mechanical, photocopying, recording, or otherwise, without permission of the publisher. For information regarding permission, write to Scholastic Inc., 557 Broadway, New York, NY 10012-3999.

Cover design by Jason Robinson

Interior design by Sydney Wright

Interior illustrations by Teresa Anderko

ISBN-13: 978-0-439-62917-1
ISBN-10: 0-439-62917-9
Text copyright © 2008 by Immacula A. Rhodes
Illustrations copyright © 2008 by Scholastic Inc.
Published by Scholastic Inc.
All rights reserved.
Printed in the U.S.A.

4 5 6 7 8 9 10   40   15 14 13

Contents

Introduction 5

    About the Games and Activities 6

    Management Tips 6

    Expanding the Use of the Games 7

    Connections to the Language Arts Standards 7

Games and Activities

Sentence Shopping Spree (*Types of Sentences*) 8

Switch-a-Subject Sentences (*Parts of a Sentence: Subjects and Predicates*) . . 11

Sentence Roundup (*Parts of a Sentence: Subjects and Predicates*) 13

Conjunction Monkeys (*Conjunctions*) 18

Conjunction Connection (*Conjunctions*) 21

"Punch-uation" Station (*Punctuation: Sentence Endings*) . . . 25

Pop-Up Punctuation (*Punctuation: Sentence Endings*) 28

Comma Cuties (*Punctuation: Commas*) 31

Quotation Queen (*Punctuation: Quotation Marks*) 34

Wheel of Quotations (*Punctuation: Quotation Marks*) 37

Captain Capital (*Capitalization*) 42

Dr. Grammar (*Capitalization and Punctuation*) 45

Noun Stackers (*Common and Proper Nouns*) 47

Pronoun Porcupine (*Singular and Plural Personal Pronouns*) 49

The Pronoun Is Right! (*Singular, Plural, and Possessive Pronouns*) 51

Ownership Octopus (*Possessive Nouns and Pronouns*) 56

What's That Noun? (*Common Nouns, Proper Nouns, and Pronouns*) 59

Planet Plural (*Regular and Irregular Noun Plurals*) 65

Nifty Noun Magic (*Irregular Noun Plurals*) 69

Verb Viper (*Regular Verbs: Present, Past, and Future Tense*) 71

Verb Match-Ups (*Irregular Verbs: Present and Past Tense*) 76

Verb-fection (*Regular and Irregular Verbs: Present and Past Tense*) 79

"To Be" Cube (*Helping and Linking Verbs*) 85

Flip-Flop Agreement Book (*Noun-Verb Agreement*) 88

Agreement Gears (*Singular and Plural Noun-Verb Agreement*) 92

Giant "I-Glasses" (*Pronoun-Verb Agreement*) 97

Adjective Hatch (*Adjectives*) 101

Zany-Zoo Adjective Game (*Adjectives*) 103

Tell-More Toad (*Adverbs*) 107

How Now? (*Adverbs*) 111

Modify Pie (*Adjectives and Adverbs*) 115

Shark Search (*Parts of Speech*) 119

Pick-Up Sticks (*Parts of Speech*) 123

Hands Down! (*Prepositions*) 125

Articles in the Attic (*Articles*) 131

Contraction Reaction (*Contractions*) 135

Katydid, Katydidn't (*Contractions With* Not) 140

Introduction

Liven up average, everyday grammar lessons with the fresh, fun-filled, learning experiences found in *Grammar Games & Activities That Boost Writing Skills*. From punctuation, capitalization, and sentence structure to parts of speech, subject-verb agreement, and contractions, the age-appropriate learning games and activities are designed to give students practical, hands-on experiences that will motivate them to strengthen and master essential writing and speaking skills.

In Sentence Shopping Spree, for example, students shop for and sort a variety of sentences. They perform first-aid on injured sentences, dates, and personal titles in Dr. Grammar and make Giant "I-Glasses" to practice agreement between pronouns and verbs. And in addition to playing new, unique games like Planet Plural, Articles in the Attic, and the Zany-Zoo Adjective Game, students will discover some familiar games played with a creative twist, such as What's That Noun?, Verb-fection, Shark Search, and Hands Down! Features and uses of the activities and games in this book follow:

- Each easy-to-make project can be assembled from the provided reproducibles and/or common classroom materials. Most of the materials needed are items found right in the classroom.

- You can use the games and activities in this collection in any order you like. Simply check the label at the top of each lesson to see the focus skill or concept.

- The activities can be done with the whole class, but most are also perfect for students to use in a learning center, either independently, with partners, or in small groups.

- Store the games in a reading center and encourage students to play before or after school, during free choice time, or when they have finished other tasks.

- You can also send games home for students to play with family members and friends.

- Extension Activity and Extending the Game ideas offer suggestions for continuing to build students' skills and interest.

- And to see how the games and activities in this book correlate with the language arts standards, see page 7.

Whether focusing on punctuation, possessives, or parts of speech, students will grow in enthusiasm and confidence as they engage in these totally terrific hands-on activities that take the *ho-hum* out of learning grammar skills and help them become better writers and speakers.

About the Games and Activities

For each game and activity, you'll find a list of materials needed, step-by-step preparation instructions, a mini-lesson for introducing the focus skill, and an extension activity to help reinforce learning. The games also include student directions for play, reproducible game boards, game cards, scorecards, game markers, and other related game pieces. To prepare most of the games, you only need markers and scissors. Accessories needed to play some of the games include readily available items such as a number cube, coin, and large, dried beans.

At the end of the lesson for each activity, you'll see the Grammar Guide icon (a boy or girl tour guide). The Grammar Guide introduces new grammar rules and provides expanded explanations or information about rules that have already been introduced. For games, the Grammar Guide appears on the reproducible playing instructions students will use.

Management Tips

The following are a few general tips to help make preparation, use, and storage a breeze.

© Prepare the games and activities ahead of time or invite students to help you make them.

© Laminate the manipulatives, game boards, and game pieces to enhance sturdiness and durability.

© Store each assembled game, game pieces, and the student directions in a gallon-sized self-sealing plastic bag. Or tape the sides of a file folder to create a large pocket in which to store the games. Use a permanent marker to write the name of the game on the plastic bag or file folder.

© Keep the games in a handy place, such as in a vertical file tray, file box, or file cabinet; on a bookshelf; or in a basket in the reading resource center.

© Conduct mini-lessons to review the grammar skills used in each activity and game.

© Model for students how to do the activity or play each game.

© For the games, give students suggestions on how to determine the order in which players take turns, such as rolling a die and taking turns in numerical order.

Expanding the Use of the Games

With just a few simple modifications, you can expand the usefulness of many of the games. For example, you can create additional sets of game cards—or even increase the difficulty level—by masking the words on the game cards and writing in your own words. In addition to creating new game cards, you can change the target skill for some games. By modifying the following games as suggested, you can use them to reinforce different skills. Feel free, of course, to modify any game as you desire to broaden its usefulness and to target specific grammar skills.

◆ Replace the words on the Conjunction Connection cards with contractions (or any other part of speech you desire).

◆ Reinforce students' knowledge of verb tenses by changing What's That Noun? to What's That Verb? and preparing cards labeled with verbs in the present, past, and future tenses.

◆ Change Verb-fection to Noun-fection. Simply replace the words on the game board with singular nouns and the words on the game cards with the corresponding plural nouns.

◆ For Hands Down!, create new cards to reinforce a different part of speech, such as nouns, verbs, adjectives, or adverbs. You might use specific types of nouns or verbs, such as singular or plural nouns, or regular or irregular verbs.

◆ Change the words on the Contraction Reaction game cards to singular and plural nouns, or present and past tense verbs.

Connections to the Language Arts Standards

The activities in this book help prepare students to meet the following standards outlined by Mid-Content Research for Education and Learning (McRel), a nationally recognized nonprofit organization that compiles and synthesizes national and state K–12 standards in languages arts, among other curriculum areas.

Uses grammatical and mechanical conventions in written compositions and uses the stylistic and rhetorical aspects of writing:

• uses declarative and interrogative sentences

• uses pronouns (e.g., substitutes pronouns for nouns, uses pronoun agreement)

• uses nouns (e.g., uses plural and singular name words, forms regular and irregular plurals of nouns, uses common and proper nouns, uses nouns as subjects)

• uses verbs (e.g., uses a wide variety of action verbs, past and present verb tenses, simple tenses, forms of regular verbs, verbs that agree with the subject)

• uses adjectives (e.g., indefinite, numeral, predicate adjectives)

• uses adverbs in written compositions (e.g., to make comparisons)

• uses coordinating conjunctions (e.g., links ideas using connecting words)

• uses conventions of capitalization (e.g., first word of a sentence; first and last names; titles of people; proper nouns [names of towns, cities, counties, and states; days of the week]; months of the year; names of streets; names of countries; holidays; first word of direct quotations; heading, salutation, and closing of a letter)

• uses conventions of punctuation (e.g., periods after declarative and imperative sentences and in initials, abbreviations, and titles before names; question marks after interrogative questions; commas in a series of words, dates and addresses and after greetings and closings in a letter; apostrophes in contractions and possessive nouns; quotation marks around titles and with direct quotations)

Source: Content Knowledge: A Compendium of Standards and Benchmarks for K–12 Education (4th ed.). *Mid-Continent Research for Education and Learning*, 2000.

Sentence Shopping Spree

Send students on a shopping spree with these special sentence-sorting carts.

SKILL

Types of Sentences

Materials

- shopping cart pattern (page 10)
- crayons or colored pencils
- scissors
- craft knife (for teacher use only)
- glue
- construction paper
- 1¼-inch wide strips of paper
- fine-tip marker
- Grammar Guide (page 9)

Getting Ready

1. Copy the shopping cart pattern. Color each labeled section of the shopping cart a different color. Then color the rest of the cart and cut it out. Also, cut each of the four slits at the top of the cart.

2. Glue only the edges of the shopping cart to a sheet of construction paper, keeping the slits free of glue.

3. On each paper strip write an example of one of the four different kinds of sentences: telling, question, request (or command), or exclamation. To make the activity self-checking, color a dot on the back of each paper strip to match the color on the shopping cart for the category that the sentence belongs to.

4. Make a copy of the Grammar Guide for each student.

Introducing the Activity

1. Review with students the information in the Grammar Guide that tells about the different kinds of sentences.

2. Have students read each sentence, decide which sentence category it belongs to, and slip the paper strip into the corresponding slit on the shopping cart.

3. After sorting the sentences, have students check their work by comparing the dot color on the back of each paper strip to the section color on the shopping cart.

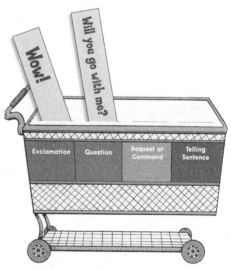

⟩ EXTENSION ACTIVITY ⟨

Telling, Telling Question!

Reinforce the different kinds of sentences with this modified game of Duck, Duck, Goose.

1. On each of 16 index cards, write a different combination of two sentence categories, such as Telling/Question, Exclamation/Command, Question/Command, or Exclamation/Telling.

2. Seat students in a circle, and appoint a student to be *It*. Secretly show *It* the sentence categories on a card (for example, Telling/Question).

3. To play:

- *It* circles the seated students, tapping each one and naming the first sentence category from the card (Telling).

- After a while, *It* calls out the second category (Question) while tapping a student. The seated student then chases *It* around the circle and back to the open space.

- The first one to reach the space sits down and calls out a sentence that fits the last named category (a question). If the sentence is appropriate, the student left standing becomes *It*. If the sentence is not appropriate, the seated student becomes *It*.

Grammar Guide

There are four kinds of sentences. Each kind has a different purpose:
- A declarative (telling) sentence makes a statement.
- An interrogative sentence asks a question.
- An imperative sentence makes a request or gives a command.
- An exclamatory sentence expresses strong feeling or emotion.

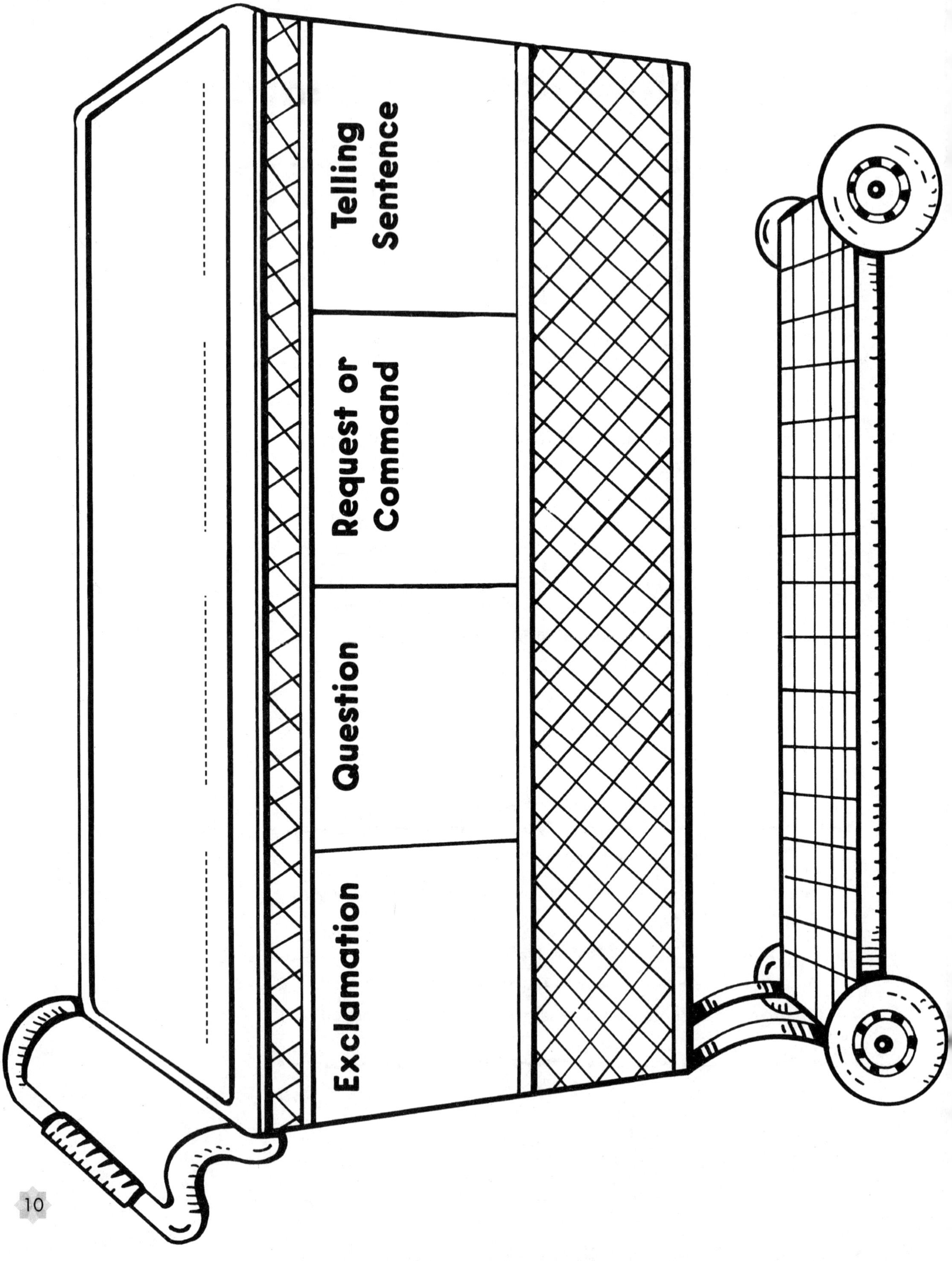

Telling Sentence

Request or Command

Question

Exclamation

Switch-a-Subject Sentences

Turn on the switch for some sentence fun! Students will enjoy switching around subjects and predicates to create new, interesting sentences.

Getting Ready

1. On sentence strips, write several declarative and exclamatory sentences about a variety of topics. (This activity works best when using sentences with either all singular-noun or all plural-noun subjects.)

2. Make a copy of the Grammar Guide for each student.

Introducing the Activity

1. Review with students the information in the Grammar Guide that tells about subjects and predicates.

2. Read each sentence with students. Together decide which part of the sentence is the subject and which is the predicate. Ask volunteers to fold each sentence strip between the two parts to divide the subject and predicate. When finished, unfold all the strips.

3. Explain that students will use the sentence strips to create new sentences by switching the subjects and predicates of two separate sentences. To use, a student picks a sentence, folds it between the subject and predicate, and places the subject faceup. Likewise, he or she folds a second sentence strip and places the predicate faceup next to the subject of the first sentence strip.

4. Have students write their new sentences on paper and illustrate them. Later, invite them to share their work with the class to compare how the different subject-predicate combinations affect sentence meanings.

SKILL

Parts of a Sentence: Subjects and Predicates

Materials

- sentence strips
- markers
- paper
- Grammar Guide (page 12)

Subject-Predicate Match-Up

Students team up for more subject and predicate practice in this fun game.

1. Divide the class into two teams: the subject team and the predicate team. Give each team member a 2-inch-wide strip of paper. Have students write only the part of a sentence that corresponds to their team designations on their paper strips. For example, students on the subject team will write only sentence subjects on their sentence strips.

2. Have the teams line up and face each other. On a signal, the first player on the subject team searches the predicate team's papers to find an appropriate predicate for his or her subject.
- If a match is found, both players place their paper strips together in an open area of the floor and then sit down.
- If no match can be made, the player goes to the end of his or team's line.

3. On the next turn, a member of the predicate team searches for an appropriate subject for his or her predicate. Continue alternating turns between the teams until each player has had a turn or has had a chance to include his or her paper strip in a sentence.

4. When all possible matches have been made, review the sentences created by team members. Afterward, have students claim their paper strips, rearrange their positions on their teams, and play again.

Grammar Guide

A sentence is made up of two parts: a subject and a predicate.
- The subject tells who or what a sentence is about. It can include a person, place, thing, or idea.
- The predicate tells something about the subject. It tells what the subject is (or was) or does (or did).

Sentence Roundup

Students put subjects and predicates together to make complete sentences.

Getting Ready

1. Copy the game directions, a game board for each player, and the game card page.

2. Color and laminate the game boards and the game cards. Then cut out the game components.

Introducing the Game

1. Review the following information about subjects and predicates with students:
   - The subject of a sentence tells who or what a sentence is about. It can include a person, place, thing, or idea.
   - The predicate tells something about the subject. It tells what the subject is (or was) or does (or did).
   - Both a subject and a predicate are needed to form a complete sentence.

2. Before students play the game, review the game directions and rules with them and model how to play.

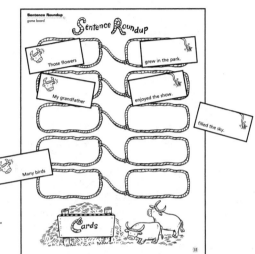

SKILL

Parts of a Sentence:
Subjects and Predicates

Materials

- game directions (page 14)
- game board (page 15)
- game cards (pages 16–17)
- colored pencils or markers
- scissors

EXTENDING THE GAME

Give students a copy of the game board. Invite them to make up their own sentences by writing a subject in each lasso on the left and a predicate in the corresponding lasso on the right. Or have students cut out sentences from newspapers, magazines, and catalogs. Have them cut apart each sentence between its subject and predicate and then glue each part in the appropriate lasso.

Sentence Roundup

Lasso subjects and predicates to make complete sentences.

Players

2 or 3

Materials

- Sentence Roundup game boards
- game cards

How to Play

1. Each player takes a game board.

2. One player shuffles the cards and places the stack facedown on the table.

3. To take a turn, a player picks two cards and reads them.

   - If the player can make a complete sentence with the cards, he or she places them on a pair of lassos. Be sure to put the subject card on the lasso on the left and the predicate card on the lasso on the right.

   - If a player cannot make a complete sentence with the cards, he or she puts them facedown on the haystack on the game board.

4. When the last card in the main stack is used, one player gathers the cards on each player's haystack and shuffles them. Players use this stack of cards to continue the game.

5. The first player to fill in all of his or her lasso pairs with complete sentences is the winner!

Hint

Subject cards have a cow's head on them; predicate cards have a cow's tail.

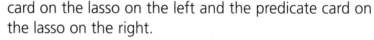

Grammar Guide

- The *subject* tells who or what a sentence is about. It can include a person, place, thing, or idea.

- The *predicate* tells something about the subject. It tells what the subject is (or was) or does (or did).

Grammar Games & Activities That Boost Writing Skills © 2008 by Immacula A. Rhodes. Scholastic Teaching Resources

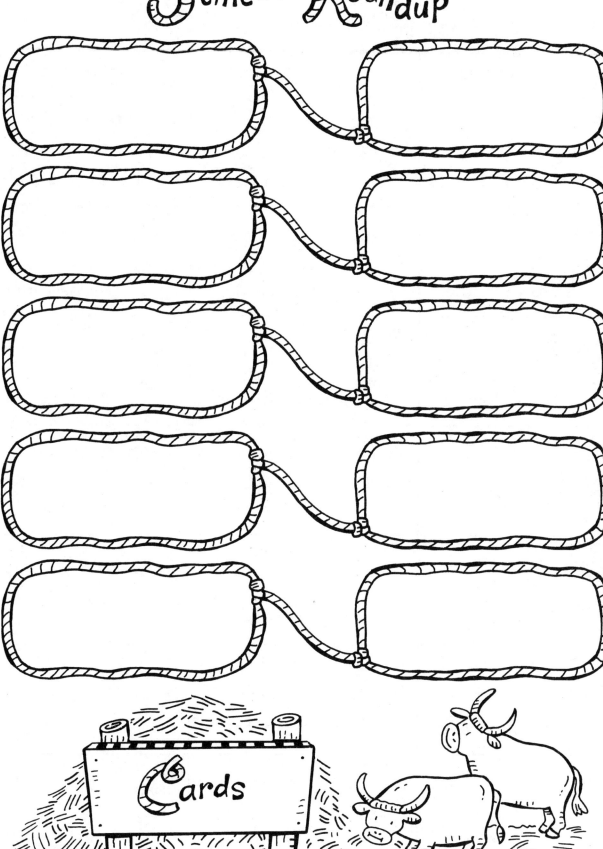

Grammar Games & Activities That Boost Writing Skills © 2008 by Immacula A. Rhodes. Scholastic Teaching Resources

Four goats	Her silly family	Our school bus
The big red ball	Bright stars	The boys and girls
One brown mouse	The teacher	His best friend
Those flowers	A police officer	The little lamp
The students	Our dog	The book
Goldilocks	Many birds	They
The busy bees	My grandfather	We
The baby	Everybody	The marching band

Grammar Games & Activities That Boost Writing Skills © 2008 by Immacula A. Rhodes. Scholastic Teaching Resources

crossed the bridge.	jumped into the pool.	rolled down the hill.
bounced up and down.	lit up the night.	played on the beach.
hid in the garden.	went home after school.	watched T.V.
grew in the park.	stood by the door.	looked very pretty.
ate fish for lunch.	chased a rabbit.	fell on the floor.
slept in the bed.	filled the sky.	laughed at the clown.
hurried off to work.	drank some milk.	stopped at the store.
smiled.	enjoyed the show.	made a loud noise.

Grammar Games & Activities That Boost Writing Skills © 2008 by Immacula A. Rhodes. Scholastic Teaching Resources

Conjunction Monkeys

With the help of these funky monkeys, students will really get into the swing of using conjunctions to create compound sentences.

SKILL

Conjunctions

Materials

- Conjunction Monkey patterns (page 20)
- crayons
- scissors
- sentence strips
- craft knife (for teacher use only)
- markers
- Grammar Guide (page 19)

Getting Ready

1. Copy and color the conjunction monkey patterns. Glue each one to tagboard and cut it out. Laminate all the pieces.

2. Write a sentence on each sentence strip, then trim the strip close to the last word. Mid-length on each sentence strip, cut a 1-inch-wide slit about ½-inch from the top and bottom edges.

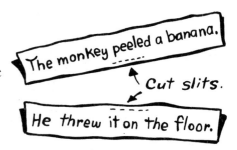

3. Make a copy of the Grammar Guide for each student.

Introducing the Activity

1. Review with students the information in the Grammar Guide that tells how conjunctions are used.

2. Invite students to select two sentence strips. Then have them connect the sentences with a conjunction monkey by hooking its upper arm into the bottom slit of one sentence strip and its lower arm in the top slit of the other.

3. Tell students to write their new compound sentences on paper. Remind them to replace the period in the first sentence with a comma and to use a lowercase letter for the first word of the second sentence. Invite students to illustrate their sentences.

Conjunction Can

Use these labeled craft sticks to reinforce students' recognition of conjunctions and sharpen their listening skills.

1. Cover a short chip canister with construction paper and label it "Conjunction Can." Write *or, and,* or *but* on the ends of a supply of craft sticks.

2. Tell students that conjunctions not only connect two or more sentences, but they also link words and phrases together. Then give student pairs a passage to read. As the first student reads aloud, ask the partner to listen for conjunctions in the passage. Each time a conjunction is read, have the partner place a corresponding stick in the Conjunction Can.

3. When finished, have the second student read the passage aloud while his or her partner listens for the conjunctions. This time, whenever the reader reaches a conjunction, the partner removes a corresponding stick from the can.

4. By the end of the passage, all of the sticks should have been removed from the can. If desired, conclude by having both partners review the passage to count each type of conjunction contained in it.

Grammar Guide

Two or more sentences can be joined together with a conjunction.

- The three most common conjunctions are *and, or,* and *but.*
- When one sentence is connected to another, a compound sentence is formed.
- A comma and a conjunction are used between the two connecting sentences.

and

or

but

Conjunction Connection

Students try to get four conjunctions in a row to win the game.

Getting Ready

1. Copy and cut out the game board.

2. Copy the game cards in two different colors.

3. Laminate the game board and game cards.

4. Cut apart the game cards and place each color in a separate bag.

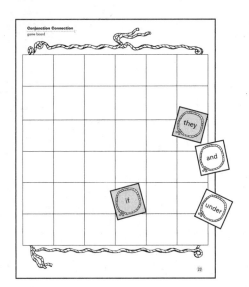

SKILL

Conjunctions

Materials

- game directions (page 22)
- two colors of copy paper
- game board (page 23)
- game cards (page 24)
- scissors
- two self-sealing plastic sandwich bags

Introducing the Game

1. Review with students the following information about conjunctions:
   - Conjunctions join two or more words together.
   - The most common conjunctions are *and, or,* and *but.* Other conjunctions are *for, if,* and *until.*

2. Before students play the game, review the game directions and rules with them and model how to play.

EXTENDING THE GAME

Give small groups a bag containing only the conjunction cards. Have students draw a card from the bag and read the word on it. Ask them to search magazines, newspapers, posters, and other print around the room to find three to five sentences that use the conjunction. Invite them to share their findings with the group.

Conjunction Connection

Get four conjunctions in a row to win the game.

Grammar Games & Activities That Boost Writing Skills © 2008 by Immacula A. Rhodes. Scholastic Teaching Resources

Players

2

Materials

- Conjunction Connection game board
- game cards (contained in 2 bags)

Hint

A player can also use any card to block the other player from getting four cards in a row.

How to Play

1. Each player chooses a bag of colored game cards.

2. To take a turn, a player picks a card, reads the word, and decides if it is a conjunction.

game cards in bags

- If it is a conjunction, the player places it on a box at the bottom of the game board.
- If not, the player sets the card aside.

3. The second player repeats step 2 but places a conjunction card on an empty box on the bottom row or in the box just above the first player's card.

4. Players take turns, each time placing a card in a box either beside or above cards that are already on the board. (Always move from the bottom of the board to the top.)

5. The first player to get four conjunction cards in a row (across, down, or diagonally) calls out, "Conjunction Connection!" and the game ends.

Grammar Guide

- Conjunctions join two or more words together.
- The most common conjunctions are *and, or,* and *but.*
- Other conjunctions are *for, if,* and *until.*

and	but	or	for	if	until
and	but	or	for	if	until
and	but	or	for	if	until
you	she	he	they	we	I
under	over	behind	beside	above	near
late	early	here	there	now	then

"Punch-uation" Station

All Aboard! Invite students to chug along on a scavenger hunt to find those often overlooked sentence-enders: the period, question mark, and exclamation point.

Getting Ready

1. Copy and cut out the train cards.

2. Make a copy of the Grammar Guide for each student.

SKILL

Punctuation:
Sentence Endings

Introducing the Activity

1. Review examples of telling sentences, questions, and exclamations with students. Discuss why each sentence ends with its particular punctuation mark.

2. Divide the class into small groups. Ask each group to color its train card.

3. Have each group assemble itself into a human train. Give the train card and a hole punch to each train's engineer and a clipboard, paper, and pencil to the train's caboose.

4. Send the trains on a punctuation scavenger hunt around the school. As they chug along, instruct students to search the walls, displays, message boards, and other visible print materials to find examples of sentences ending in periods, question marks, and exclamation points.

5. Each time the group finds a sentence that ends with a mark on the train card, have the engineer punch a hole in the corresponding section of the card. Then have the caboose write that sentence on paper.

6. After a designated time, direct the trains back to the station (classroom). Have the groups compare and share their findings for each type of punctuation.

Materials

- train card, one per small group (page 27)
- scissors
- colored pencils or markers
- hole punch (one per small group)
- clipboard (one per small group)
- paper
- pencil
- Grammar Guide (page 26)

Punch holes.

The art contest begins next week.
The Maple Street Mustangs won the Spelling Bee!
Do you need extra help with your homework?

All Aboard the Sentence Train!

Keep students on track learning about sentence-ending punctuation with this activity.

1. Solicit help from students to decorate three shoe boxes to resemble trains. Label each with a type of punctuation: period, question mark, or exclamation point.

2. Put the trains in the writing center along with a supply of paper slips. Then post several signs labeled with different topics of study or interest to students (science, sports, TV shows).

3. Have students visit the center to write a telling, question, and exclamation sentence about the topics, each on a separate slip of paper. Ask them to put their papers into the corresponding train.

4. Later, invite volunteers to select slips from each train and read the examples to the class.

Grammar Guide

Every sentence ends with a punctuation mark.

- A period ends a telling (or declarative) sentence.
- A question mark ends a question (also called an asking or interrogative sentence).
- An exclamation point ends an exclamation (or exclamatory sentence).

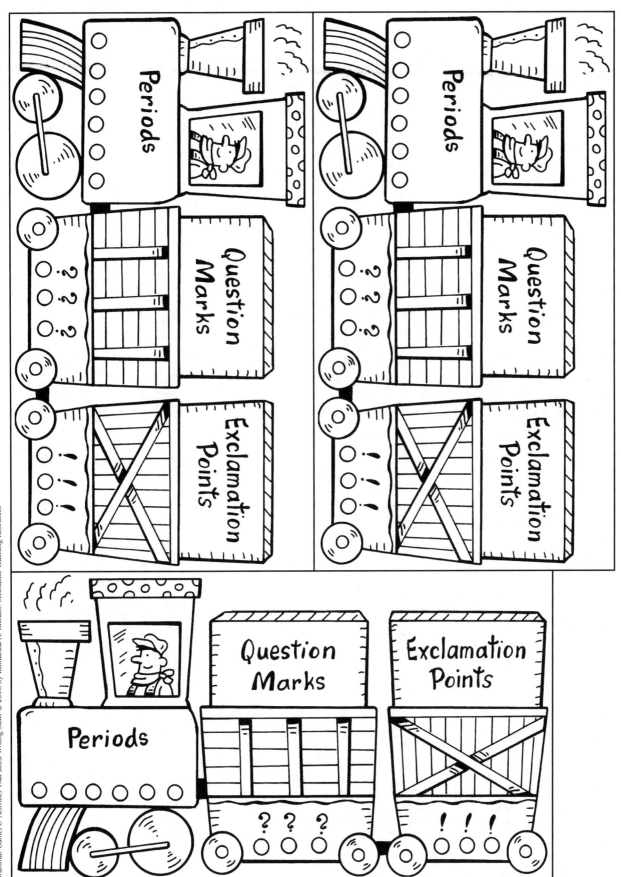

Grammar Games & Activities That Boost Writing Skills © 2008 by Immacula A. Rhodes. Scholastic Teaching Resources

Pop-Up Punctuation

Students will pop sentence-ending punctuation right into place with these special pop-up cards.

SKILL

Punctuation:
Sentence Endings

Materials

- punctuation and stand patterns (page 30)
- crayons or colored pencils
- scissors
- craft knife (for teacher use only)
- glue
- sentence strips
- markers
- sticky dots in three colors
- Grammar Guide (page 29)

Teaching Tip

- You might wish to glue the cards to tagboard to make them sturdier.

- If desired, make a pair of sentence strip stands (as shown) from 7½-inch lengths of sentence strips. To use, place a sentence strip in the stands.

Getting Ready

1. Copy the pattern page and color the punctuation patterns. Then laminate, if desired.

2. Cut out the punctuation patterns and cards. Then cut the slits in each card.

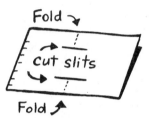

3. Fold the cards, as shown. Open each one so that it stands at a 90° angle.

4. Glue a punctuation mark to the pop-out section of each card. After the glue dries, close the cards.

5. Write different kinds of sentences and interjections on sentence strips, omitting the ending punctuation from each. Trim each strip close to the last word.

6. To make the activity self-checking, affix a different color sticky dot to each punctuation card. Then stick a matching dot to the back of each sentence strip labeled with a sentence that uses the corresponding punctuation mark.

7. Make a copy of the Grammar Guide for each student.

Introducing the Activity

1. Review with students examples of telling sentences, questions, exclamations, commands, and interjections, as well as the different types of punctuation used for each. (See Grammar Guide, below.)

2. Give pairs or small groups of students the sentence strips and punctuation cards (and stands, if applicable). Have them read each sentence strip, decide which punctuation mark to use, and then "pop" open and place the corresponding card at the end of the sentence strip.

3. Invite them to check their answers by comparing the color dots on the cards and sentence strips.

◀ ---------------------- ▶ **EXTENSION ACTIVITY** ◀ ---------------------- ▶

Sentence-Ender Show-Off

This quick-and-easy activity helps students show off what they know about sentence-ending punctuation.

1. Have students draw a large period, question mark, and exclamation point, each on a separate half-sheet of paper.

2. Write a sentence on the chalkboard, omitting the ending punctuation. Ask students to read the sentence, decide which punctuation should end the sentence, and hold the corresponding paper overhead.

3. Fill in the correct punctuation mark. Have students check and discuss their answers.

Grammar Guide

Commands and interjections also end with punctuation.

- A period ends a gentle command (or imperative sentence), such as "Write your name on your paper."

- An exclamation point ends a strong command (or imperative sentence), such as "Throw the ball to first base!"

- An exclamation point ends an interjection (words that show strong feelings, such as "Ouch!" or "Hooray!").

Comma Cuties

Put comma confusion to rest! Use these little cuties to help students learn comma placement in sentences, addresses, and dates.

Getting Ready

1. Copy and glue the comma cutie and crib patterns to tagboard. Then color and cut out each one. If desired, laminate the pieces.

2. Cut the slits in the crib.

3. Back each comma cutie and the crib with magnetic tape.(Affix magnetic tape to each corner of the crib.)

4. Insert each comma cutie into a slit in the crib. Place the crib on a magnetic chalkboard.

5. In large handwriting on the chalkboard, write a variety of sentences, dates, addresses, and phrases requiring the use of commas. Omit each comma in the examples, leaving enough space to fit a comma cutie in its position.

6. Make a copy of the Grammar Guide for each student.

SKILL

Punctuation: Commas

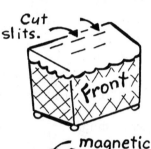

Cut slits.

Front

magnetic tape

Back

Insert comma cutie in each slot.

Materials

- Comma Cutie and crib patterns (page 33)
- tagboard
- glue
- colored pencils or markers
- scissors
- craft knife (for teacher use only)
- magnetic tape
- magnetic chalkboard (or magnet board)
- Grammar Guide (page 32)

Introducing the Activity

1. Review with students the information in the Grammar Guide about how commas are used. Then point out one of the sentence examples on the chalkboard. Ask students to determine where one or more commas belong in it. Have a student remove comma cuties from the crib and place them where commas are needed in the example.

2. Next, students read the example with the comma cuties in place. Remind them to pause briefly at the comma before reading the next word.

Alan ate a hamburger, hot dog, and piece of cake. He said, "I feel sick."

Place the comma cuties.

31

EXTENSION ACTIVITY

Crafty Commas

Invite students to use simple craft items as tools for learning about comma placement.

1. On the chalkboard write examples of sentences, dates, addresses, and phrases requiring the use of commas (be sure to omit the commas). Provide students with manipulative commas: elbow macaroni, the bendable sections of elbow straws, or short curved lengths of pipe cleaners.

2. Invite volunteers to hold their manipulative commas in the spaces where commas belong in the examples. Then ask the class to chorally read each example, pausing briefly at each comma before continuing to the next word.

3. Later, write similar comma-containing examples on sentence strips, omitting the commas. Ask students to place a comma manipulative on the examples wherever a comma is needed.

4. Finally, have students write their own examples—including the commas—to share with the class.

Grammar Guide

A comma separates words, phrases, or clauses. When reading, pause (or rest) briefly at each comma.

A comma separates:

- a series of three or more words or phrases.
- clauses in a sentence.
- a direct quote from the rest of the sentence.

A comma is placed between:

- a city and state name.
- the day and year in a date.

A comma is placed after the greeting and closing of a friendly letter.

Quotation Queen

Provide regal reinforcement in using quotation marks with this queen's crown jewels.

SKILL

Punctuation:
Quotation Marks

Materials

- queen and quotation mark patterns (page 36)
- colored pencils or markers
- scissors
- glue
- magnetic tape
- magnetic chalkboard (or wipe-off board)
- wipe-off markers (if using a wipe-off board)
- Grammar Guide (page 35)

Getting Ready

1. Copy, color, and cut out the queen and quotation mark patterns. Laminate all the pieces.

2. Back each quotation mark with magnetic tape. Also, stick a length of magnetic tape behind the row of quotation marks on the crown.

3. Attach the individual quotation-mark "jewels" to the corresponding marks on the front of the crown. (The magnets will hold them in place.)

4. Place the queen on a magnetic chalkboard.

5. Draw a large speech bubble near the queen. Inside the bubble, write a quote from the queen.

6. Make a copy of the Grammar Guide for each student.

Put quotation mark jewels on crown.

Introducing the Activity

1. Review with students the information in the Grammar Guide about how quotation marks are used.

2. Demonstrate how quotation marks are used to set off a person's words when written. Explain that the words inside the bubble are the queen's exact words. Invite a student to remove the individual quotation-mark jewels from the queen's crown and place them around the words in the speech bubble. Then have the student erase the outline of the speech bubble.

Add quotation mark jewels.

We're having a castle party tomorrow.

Erase speech bubble.

3. To complete the sentence, have the student add a speaker reference before or after the quote, setting it off with a comma. (Refer to the Grammar Guide on page 32 for comma rules.) Then ask the student to read the sentence aloud.

4. Have the students return the quotation-mark jewels to the queen's crown. Then erase the quote and repeat steps 2–3 as often as necessary to give each student the opportunity to create a quotation.

5. To provide practice in setting off titles, write sentences that contain titles of magazine and newspaper articles, and song and poem titles. Have students take turns placing the quotation-mark jewels around the titles.

EXTENSION ACTIVITY

Craft-Spoon Quotations

Use these unique manipulatives to spoon up a helping of wholesome practice in using quotation marks.

1. Glue wooden craft spoons together, as shown, to create a pair of quotation marks. Back each set of marks with magnetic tape.

2. On a magnetic chalkboard (or wipe-off board) write sentences that contain direct quotes or titles that should be set off with quotation marks. Be sure to omit the quotation marks.

3. Invite students to place the spoon quotation marks around the quotes and titles in each sentence. Ask them to explain why they placed the marks in the positions they did.

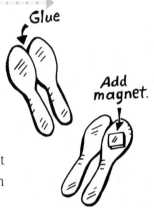

Grammar Guide

Quotation marks come in pairs. They are used to set off quotes and some titles from the rest of a sentence. Quotation marks are placed before and after:

 ▪ a direct quote (the exact words spoken by a person or character).

 ▪ titles of magazine and newspaper articles, and song and poem titles.

Wheel of Quotations

Students tell when and where a sentence needs quotations marks.

Getting Ready

1. Copy the game directions and the game card pages. Then copy the game board onto tagboard and color it.

2. Laminate the game board and a copy of the game card pages.

3. Cut the slits on the wheel. Then cut apart the cards. Carefully fold back and crease the bottom part of each card.

4. Copy and cut out a supply of scorecards.

Introducing the Game

1. Review with students the following rules about how quotation marks are used:
   - Quotation marks are placed before and after a direct quote.
   - A punctuation mark found at the end of a direct quote goes inside the quotation marks.

2. Before students play the game, review the game rules and directions with them and model how to play.

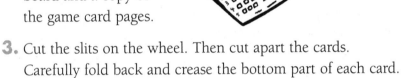

folded game card in each slot

I fell down, cried Dan.

Add quotation marks if needed.

wheel

SKILL

Punctuation: Quotation Marks

Materials

- game directions (page 38)
- tagboard
- game board (page 39)
- scorecard (page 40)
- game cards (pages 40–41)
- colored pencils or markers
- scissors
- craft knife (for teacher use only)
- large paper clip
- pencils
- wipe-off marker

EXTENDING THE GAME

Ask students to pick a card, read it, and draw a picture to represent the sentence. To do this, they draw the character that the sentence is about, add a speech bubble, and write the character's words in it. If the sentence does not have a direct quote, students can make up a sentence to write in the bubble.

Wheel of Quotations

Earn points by telling when and where to add quotations marks.

Players

2–3

Materials

- Wheel of Quotations game board
- game cards
- scorecards
- large paper clip
- pencils
- wipe-off marker

How to Play

1. Each player writes his or her name on a scorecard. One player puts a game card, folded side down, in each slit on the game board.

2. To take a turn, a player spins the spinner, removes the card the spinner lands on, reads the sentence, and answers the question, "Are quotation marks needed?" If the player answers "yes," he or she uses the wipe-off pen to fill in the marks where they belong. The player then unfolds the card and checks the sentence at the bottom to see if he or she is correct.

   - If the sentence needs quotation marks and the player filled them in correctly, he or she writes 10 in the "Yes" and "Bonus" boxes on the scorecard.

   - If the player did not fill in the quotation marks correctly, he or she writes 10 in the "Yes" box only.

   - If the sentence does not need quotation marks and the player answered correctly, he or she writes 10 in the "No" box.

3. The player puts a new card in the open slit on the game board and play continues. When no cards are left to fill the slits, players spin until they land on a space with a card.

4. After his or her scorecard is filled in, each player adds the score. The player with the highest score wins!

Fold game cards along dotted line.

I fell down, cried Dan.

"I fell down," cried Dan.

Place each card in slot on wheel.

game board

Grammar Guide

- Quotation marks are placed before and after a direct quote.
- A punctuation mark found at the end of a direct quote goes inside the quotation marks.

Grammar Games & Activities That Boost Writing Skills © 2008 by Immacula A. Rhodes. Scholastic Teaching Resources

Wheel of Quotations

game board

Hold pencil over paper clip.

Spin!

He said, I like milk.	Mr. Todd told me to read.
He said, "I like milk."	Mr. Todd told me to read.
Time for bed, said Mom.	The girl whispered her name.
"Time for bed," said Mom.	The girl whispered her name.
The man said, I'm hungry.	Tom asked me to play.
The man said, "I'm hungry."	Tom asked me to play.

Name: _____

Wheel of Quotations
score card

	Are " " needed?		Bonus	Score
	Yes	No		
1.	☐	☐	☐	
2.	☐	☐	☐	
3.	☐	☐	☐	
4.	☐	☐	☐	
5.	☐	☐	☐	
6.	☐	☐	☐	

Total _____

Grammar Games & Activities That Boost Writing Skills © 2008 by Immacula A. Rhodes. Scholastic Teaching Resources

I love to dance, said Jen.	Please tell me the answer.
"I love to dance," said Jen.	Please tell me the answer.
The coach yelled, Time out!	I told her we had fun.
The coach yelled, "Time out!"	I told her we had fun.
Today is Monday, said Dad.	The teacher spoke softly.
"Today is Monday," said Dad.	The teacher spoke softly.
I fell down, cried Dan.	Mary shouted at us.
"I fell down," cried Dan.	Mary shouted at us.
That's my dog, said Mia.	I said that I felt sick.
"That's my dog," said Mia.	I said that I felt sick.
The boy shouted, Let's race!	She told us to sit down.
The boy shouted, "Let's race!"	She told us to sit down.

Captain Capital

Invite students to join this caped superhero in some challenging capital capers.

SKILL

Capitalization

Materials

- Captain Capital pattern, one per student (page 44)
- crayons or colored pencils
- newspapers, magazines, department store flyers, junk mail letters, and other disposable print materials
- scissors
- glue sticks
- Grammar Guide (page 43)

Getting Ready

Make a copy of the Captain Capital pattern and the Grammar Guide for each student.

Introducing the Activity

1. Review with students the rules in the Grammar Guide for using commas and then give a few examples.

2. Give each student a copy of the Captain Capital pattern to color.

3. Provide students with magazines, newspapers, department store flyers, junk mail letters, and other disposable print materials to search for words that follow the capitalization rules. Instruct them to cut out only the words that follow the rules. (Caution students to avoid the many words that use all capital letters, such as in advertisements and store names. You might take this opportunity to brainstorm and discuss reasons why some words are printed in all capital letters.)

4. Have students glue the correctly capitalized words to Captain Capital's cape.

5. Invite students to share the words on their superhero's cape with the class.

Class Capitalization Cape

Make this collaborative class cape that reinforces capitalization skills while allowing students to share information about themselves.

1. Spread a white, twin-size flat sheet (or similar size piece of cloth) on a table or the floor.

2. Invite students to use paint pens to write on the sheet personal and interesting facts about themselves, such as their names, city and state of birth, birth month and day, and titles of their favorite books, movies, or songs. Encourage them to capitalize each entry they make on the sheet correctly. If space allows, also have them illustrate their entries.

3. Afterward, invite one student at a time to drape the sheet—or cape— around his or her shoulders and name a few personal entries written on it. Challenge the class to search the cape to find the named information.

Capital letters are used at the beginning of a word. Always capitalize:

- the first word in a sentence.
- the pronoun "I."
- proper nouns, including cities, states, days of the week, and months of the year.
- official titles, such as Dr. and Mrs.
- the first word in the greeting and closing of a friendly letter.
- all the main words in titles (books, movies, songs, plays, television shows, and so on).

Capitals are used in many acronyms and abbreviations, such as in DEAR (Drop Everything and Read) and CD (compact disc).

Captain Capital pattern

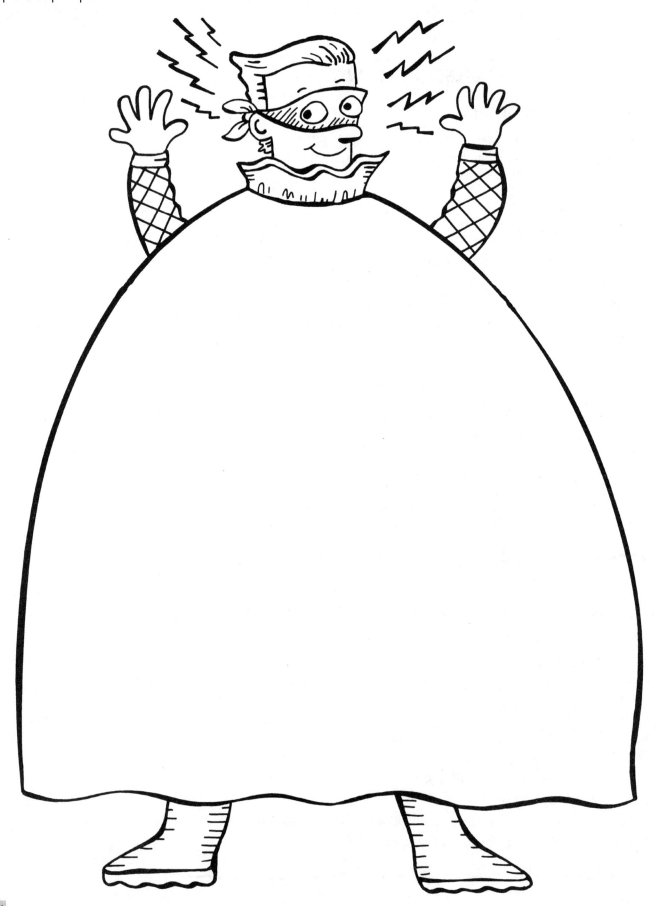

Dr. Grammar

Each young Dr. Grammar in your class can use simple medical supplies to nurse grammatically injured words, sentences, and phrases to perfect health.

Getting Ready

1. Remove the wrappers from two pairs of round spot bandages and several mini bandages. (Leave the backing on the bandages.)

2. Use the permanent marker to draw quotation marks on each pair of spot bandages. Draw a period, comma, question mark, or exclamation point on each of the mini bandages.

3. Write a large capital letter on one end of each tongue depressor. Place the tongue depressors in the wide-mouth pill bottle. (Thoroughly wash and dry the bottle first.)

spot bandages

mini bandages

4. Write a variety of sentences each on a separate strip of paper. Use lowercase letters in some places where capitals should be used. Omit the end punctuation, commas, and quotation marks in some of the sentences. Leave plenty of space where punctuation is omitted so that students can fill in the missing marks.

5. Make a copy of the Grammar Guide for each student.

Introducing the Activity

1. Review with students the rules in the Grammar Guide about capitalization and punctuation.

2. Invite a student to wear the lab coat and stethoscope (if using) and take the role of Dr. Grammar. Have the doctor

SKILL

Capitalization and Punctuation

Materials

- small, round (spot) adhesive bandages
- mini (3/8-inch wide) adhesive bandages
- 26 (or more) tongue depressors (or wide craft sticks)
- fine-tip permanent marker
- large, wide-mouth pill bottle (without lid)
- two-inch-wide strips of paper
- lab coat (optional)
- toy stethoscope (optional)
- Grammar Guide (page 46)

Teaching Tip

Prepare extra sticks for sample sentences that require more than one of the same capital letter.

examine one of the sentences to find all of its injured parts. Then ask him or her to place the appropriate tongue depressors and bandages on the sentence to nurse it back to health. (Instruct Dr. Grammar to leave the backing on the bandages so that they can be used to heal other sentences.)

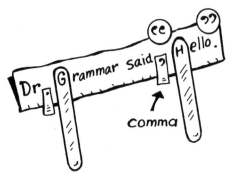

3. On additional strips of paper, write dates, names of people with personal titles, city and state names, street names, and other word groupings that require capitalization and punctuation. Invite students to role-play Dr. Grammar and to nurse these items back to health with the provided supplies.

EXTENSION ACTIVITY

Grammar Check-Up

Students write about their role-playing activities to help build healthy punctuation and capitalization skills.

1. Invite student pairs to role-play a visit to the doctor. Ask the partners to switch roles so that each student has the opportunity to be the patient.

2. Afterward, have students write about their experiences as patients, including references to the doctor (by title and name, such as Dr. Abeyta) and dialogue between the doctor and patient. As they write, remind students to use correct punctuation and capitalization.

3. When finished, ask the partners to edit each other's papers. Have students rewrite their papers, as needed, and then share them with the class.

Grammar Guide

Punctuation and capitalization work together.

- Begin every sentence with a capital letter.
- End every sentence with a punctuation mark.
- Capitalize the first word of a direct quote set off with quotation marks (in most instances).
- Capitalize the first letter of an abbreviated personal title and end it with a period (such as in Dr. and Mr.).

Noun Stackers

Students' noun knowledge will really stack up when they build this noun-high tower.

Getting Ready

1. Evenly divide the tubes into two sets. Use the permanent marker to write common nouns on one set of tubes and proper nouns on the other.

2. Place all the tubes in a box.

3. Copy the Grammar Guide for each student.

Introducing the Activity

1. Review with students the information in the Grammar Guide about common and proper nouns.

2. Give the box of tubes and a broom to a student pair. Explain that they will use these to build a tower of nouns. Then have one student hold the broom handle upright. Instruct his or her partner to search the box to find tubes labeled with either common nouns or proper nouns. Each time the student finds an example of the designated type of noun, he or she slides it onto the broom handle.

3. When the stacked tubes fill the broom handle, have students read each word on the tower to verify that it is an example of the designated type of noun: common or proper.

4. Ask students to return the tubes to the box. Then have them switch roles to build the next tower.

SKILL

Common and Proper Nouns

Materials

- 30 (or more) 4½-inch lengths of paper towel tubes
- permanent marker
- box
- broom handle or wooden dowel
- Grammar Guide (page 48)

Tower Relay

In this friendly, fast-paced game, teams compete to build a tower of common or proper nouns.

1. Invite students to use the tube tower materials in a relay race. First, obtain a second broom, with a handle the same length as the first. Prepare extra tubes for each type of noun and add them to the box.

2. Divide the class into two teams. Line each team up at one end of the room. Appoint a member of each team to hold a broom at the opposite end of the room. Place the box of tubes in the middle.

3. To play, call out a type of noun (common or proper), and give a signal. The first player on each team races to the box, finds a tube with an appropriate noun, and continues on to place the tube onto the broom handle.

5. The student holding the broom handle checks the tube to make sure it's labeled with the right kind of noun.

  ▪ If not, the player must return to the box and pick another tube.
  ▪ If the word is acceptable, the broom-holder hands the broom to the player and then runs to tag the next player on his or her team.
  ▪ The relay continues in this manner until a team has completely filled its broom with the correct type of nouns.

A noun names a person, place, thing, or idea. Nouns can be common or proper.

  ▪ A common noun names any person, animal, place, thing, or idea.
  ▪ A common noun always begins with a lower case letter.

Unlike a common noun, a proper noun names a specific person, animal, place, thing, or idea. A proper noun always begins with a capital letter.

Pronoun Porcupine

This perky pet is the perfect pal for helping students learn about singular and plural personal pronouns.

Getting Ready

1. To make each porcupine, brush a light coat of paint onto a Styrofoam ball half. Allow the paint to dry.

2. Glue the flat side of the ball to a cardboard circle to create a dome. Glue on wiggle eyes and a pom-pom nose.

3. Use the permanent marker to write a different personal pronoun on the end of each craft stick (see the pronouns listed in Grammar Guide).

4. Poke the opposite end of each craft stick into the dome to create a porcupine with quills.

5. Make a copy of the Grammar Guide for each student.

Introducing the Activity

1. Review with students the information in the Grammar Guide about singular and plural pronouns.

2. Give students practice in recognizing plural and singular pronouns. Simply have them remove and sort the quills into two groups of personal pronouns: singular and plural.

3. To help small groups make appropriate pronoun substitutions for nouns, call out a noun. Have students tell whether the noun is singular or plural. Use the word in a sentence, then tell a student to pick a porcupine quill with

SKILL

Singular and Plural Personal Pronouns

Materials

- one half of a 3-inch Styrofoam ball
- beige acrylic paint
- paintbrush
- 3-inch cardboard circle
- craft glue
- two wiggle eyes
- black pom-pom
- 12 craft sticks
- fine-point permanent marker
- Grammar Guide (page 50)

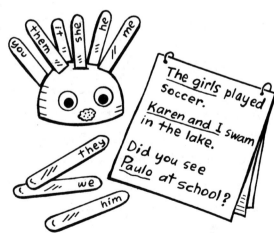

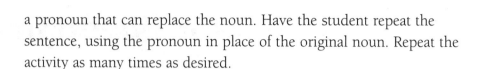

a pronoun that can replace the noun. Have the student repeat the sentence, using the pronoun in place of the original noun. Repeat the activity as many times as desired.

4. Write sentences on chart paper and underline the nouns (or noun phrases). Have students copy the sentences, replacing the underlined words with pronouns. Encourage them to refer to the pronoun porcupine when deciding which pronouns to use.

EXTENSION ACTIVITY

Spin a Noun

Use this nifty spinner to reinforce students' noun knowledge.

1. Create a freestanding triangle spinner by overlapping and gluing together the ends of a 4- by 12-inch strip of tagboard. Label each side "Common Noun," "Proper Noun," or "Pronoun." Slide the spinner onto a broom handle and lay the broom across two chairs.

2. To use, students gently spin the triangle around the broom. When it stops, they name a word that represents the type of noun shown. If the word is not a pronoun, students tell whether it can be replaced with a pronoun and what pronoun can be used to replace it.

A pronoun is a word that takes the place of a noun. Personal pronouns are the most common type of pronouns.

These personal pronouns are singular:

- *I, you, he, she, it, me, him,* and *her.*

These personal pronouns are plural:

- *we, they, us,* and *them.*

The Pronoun Is Right!

Students use pronouns to replace nouns in sentences.

Getting Ready

1. Copy the game directions, game boards, and the game card pages.

2. Color and laminate the game boards and cards. Then cut apart the cards.

3. Fold each game card in half along the dotted line. Then place each set of game cards in a separate bag.

← Fold on line.

Place cards in bag.

SKILL

Singular, Plural, and Possessive Pronouns

Materials

- game directions (page 52)
- game boards (pages 53–55)
- game cards (pages 53–55)
- colored pencils or markers
- scissors
- three paper bags

Introducing the Game

1. Review with students the following information about pronouns:
- A pronoun is a word that takes the place of a noun.
- These personal pronouns are singular: *I, you, he, she, it, me, him,* and *her.*
- These personal pronouns are plural: *we, they, us,* and *them.*
- The possessive personal pronouns are: *my, mine, your, yours, his, her, hers, its, our, ours, their,* and *theirs.*

2. Before students play the game, review the game rules and directions with them and model how to play.

EXTENDING THE GAME

Help students divide a sheet of paper into nine sections. Then have them cut out, fold, and stand a different pronoun card on each section. To use, make up and read a sentence in which a pronoun is missing. If a card with the missing pronoun is on a student's paper, have the student remove the card. Continue until a student gets three empty sections in a row.

The Pronoun Is Right!

Find pronouns that can be used in place of the underlined words in sentences.

Grammar Games & Activities That Boost Writing Skills © 2008 by Immacula A. Rhodes. Scholastic Teaching Resources

Players

2–3

Materials

- The Pronoun Is Right! game boards
- game cards (contained in 3 bags)

How to Play

1. Each player chooses a game board and a bag of game cards.

2. To take a turn, a player draws two cards from his or her bag and reads the pronouns.

3. The player then reads the first sentence and checks to see if any of the pronouns can be used in place of the underlined word or words in the sentence. If a pronoun can be used, the player stands the card on top of the word or words. The player returns the unused cards to his or her bag.

4. Once the player replaces all the underlined words in the first sentence, he or she may move to the next sentence. Each player must replace the words in their sentences in the order that they are numbered.

5. The first player to replace all the underlined words with correct pronouns is the winner!

Grammar Guide

A pronoun is a word that takes the place of a noun. Personal pronouns are the most common type of pronouns.

- These personal pronouns are singular:
  I, you, he, she, it, me, him, and *her.*

- These personal pronouns are plural:
  we, they, us, and *them.*

- The possessive personal pronouns are:
  my, mine, your, yours, his, her, hers, its, our, ours, their, and *theirs.*

The Pronoun Is Right!

game board and cards

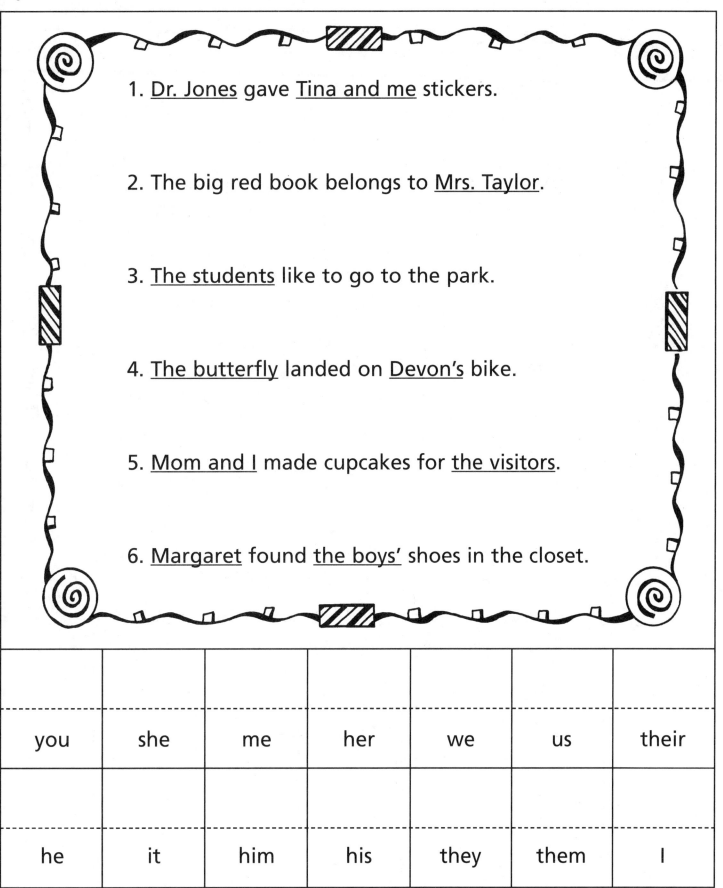

1. Dr. Jones gave Tina and me stickers.

2. The big red book belongs to Mrs. Taylor.

3. The students like to go to the park.

4. The butterfly landed on Devon's bike.

5. Mom and I made cupcakes for the visitors.

6. Margaret found the boys' shoes in the closet.

you	she	me	her	we	us	their
he	it	him	his	they	them	I

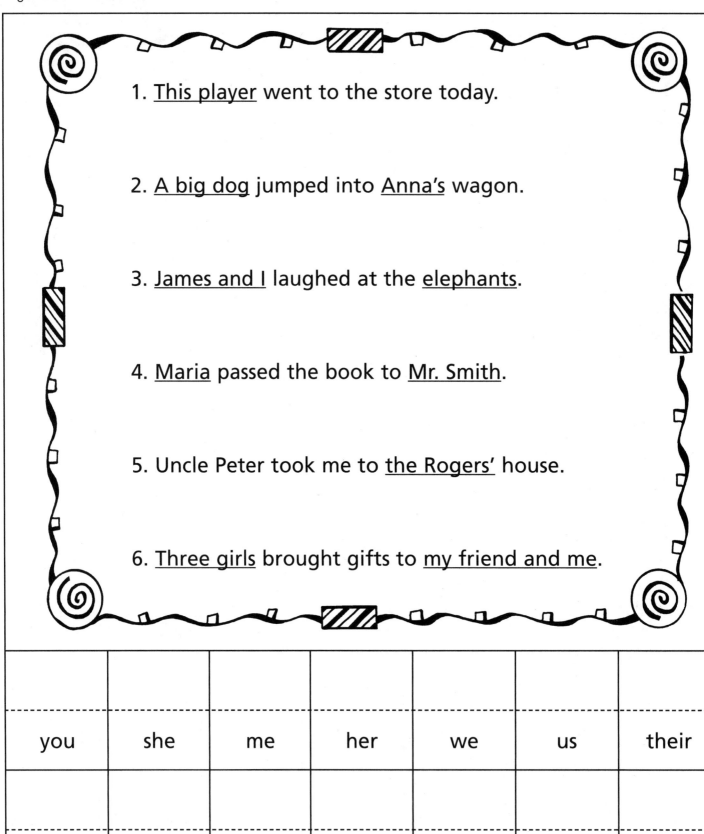

1. <u>This player</u> went to the store today.

2. <u>A big dog</u> jumped into <u>Anna's</u> wagon.

3. <u>James and I</u> laughed at the <u>elephants</u>.

4. <u>Maria</u> passed the book to <u>Mr. Smith</u>.

5. Uncle Peter took me to <u>the Rogers'</u> house.

6. <u>Three girls</u> brought gifts to <u>my friend and me</u>.

you	she	me	her	we	us	their
he	it	him	his	they	them	I

The Pronoun Is Right!

game board and cards

1. <u>The cat</u> walked across the top of the wall.

2. <u>Chad and Jill</u> took <u>Sarah</u> to the fair.

3. The wind blew <u>the girls'</u> umbrellas away.

4. <u>Fred's</u> father took <u>Fred</u> to the baseball game.

5. <u>Miss Evans</u> called <u>this player</u> on the phone.

6. <u>Don, Mia, and I</u> watched <u>the clowns</u> turn flips.

you	she	me	her	we	us	their
he	it	him	his	they	them	I

Ownership Octopus

This friendly critter is always ready to lend a hand to help students understand possessive nouns and pronouns.

SKILL

Possessive Nouns and Pronouns

Materials

- octopus pattern (page 58)
- colored pencils or markers
- tagboard
- glue
- scissors
- hole punch
- eight pieces of yarn, about 6–8 inches in length
- paper clips
- magnetic tape
- magnetic wipe-off board
- picture cutouts from magazines, catalogs, department store flyers, and other publications
- wipe-off pen
- Grammar Guide (page 57)

Getting Ready

1. To make each octopus:
   - Copy the octopus pattern and glue it to tagboard.
   - Color and laminate the pattern and then cut it out.
   - Punch a hole where indicated on each octopus arm.
   - Tape the end of a length of yarn to the back of each hole. Then thread the yarn through the hole so that it extends from the front of the octopus.
   - Tie a paper clip to the loose end of each length of yarn.
   - Back the octopus with magnetic tape. Then attach it to a magnetic wipe-off board.
   - Attach a picture cutout to each paper clip on the octopus.

2. Make a copy of the Grammar Guide for each student.

Punch hole at end of each arm.

↑Attach pictures to paper clips.

Introducing the Activity

1. Review with students the information in the Grammar Guide about possessive nouns and pronouns.

2. Use a wipe-off pen to write on the octopus a common or proper noun for a person, animal, or character.

3. To practice making possessive nouns, show each picture to students. Then have them recite the following sentences, filling in the blanks with the noun written on the octopus and the designated picture: "The (picture) belongs to (noun on octopus). It is (noun)'s (picture)." Print the possessive form of the name on the board to show students how it looks.

4. Erase the board and the noun on the octopus. Then replace the pictures on the octopus, and repeat step 3. Continue in this manner, using a variety of singular and plural nouns to reinforce students' understanding of different kinds of possessives.

5. Periodically, ask students to replace the possessive noun with a possessive pronoun. Write the pronoun on the board. Explain that apostrophes are not used in possessive pronouns.

EXTENSION ACTIVITY

My Very Own Octopus

Invite each student to make a personal octopus for more practice with possessive nouns and pronouns.

1. Have students color, cut out, and punch holes in a copy of the octopus. Then direct them to attach lengths of yarn to their cutouts, but not paper clips. Next, students write their own names on their octopuses.

2. Have students cut out pictures of objects from a variety of magazines, catalogs, sales flyers, and other publications. Tell them to tape a picture to the loose end of each yarn.

3. Finally, students write sentences about their ownership of each object pictured on their octopuses. Encourage them to correctly use and spell the possessive form of their names in their sentences.

4. If desired, display students' sentences with their octopuses. Later, ask students to rewrite their sentences, replacing their names with possessive pronouns.

Grammar Guide

Possessive nouns and pronouns tell who or what owns something.

An apostrophe is used to show a possessive noun.

- Make a singular noun possessive by adding -'s.

- If a plural noun ends in -s, just add an apostrophe to make it possessive.

- If the plural noun does not end in -s, add -'s.

Do not use apostrophes in possessive personal pronouns.

- The possessive personal pronouns are: *my, mine, your, yours, his, her, hers, its, our, ours, their,* and *theirs.*

Grammar Games & Activities That Boost Writing Skills © 2008 by Immacula A. Rhodes, Scholastic Teaching Resources

What's That Noun?

Students identify common nouns, proper nouns, and pronouns in this game based on the TV show, Jeopardy.

Getting Ready

1. Copy the game directions, game board, and the game card pages.

2. Color and laminate the game board and cards. Then cut out the game components.

3. Copy and cut apart a supply of scorecards.

Introducing the Game

1. Review with students the following information about common and proper nouns, and pronouns:

A noun names a person, place, thing, or idea. Nouns can be common or proper:

- A common noun names any person, animal, place, thing, or idea.
- A common noun always begins with a lowercase letter.
- A proper noun names a specific person, animal, place, thing, or idea.
- A proper noun always begins with a capital letter.
- A pronoun takes the place of a noun. The most common pronouns are: *I, you, he, she, it, me, him, her, we, they, us,* and *them.*

2. Before students play the game, review the game rules and directions with them and model how to play.

SKILL

Common Nouns, Proper Nouns, and Pronouns

Materials

- game directions (page 60)
- game board (page 61)
- scorecards (page 62)
- game cards (pages 63–64)
- colored pencils or markers
- scissors
- pencils

EXTENDING THE GAME

Ask students to cut apart the four rows of boxes on a copy of the game board. Have them cut slits between the boxes, starting at the bottom of each strip and stopping ½ inch from the top. Help students glue their strips onto 2- by 8-inch strips of light colored construction paper, gluing only across the top and leaving the flaps free to open and close. Tell them to write a common noun, proper noun, or pronoun under each flap. To use, a classmate lifts a flap, reads the word, and tells what kind of noun it is. Students might add the points for their correct guesses—just for extra fun!

Cut slits between each box.

radio 300 500 200

2" x 8" colored paper strip

What's That Noun?

Use a question to identify common nouns, proper nouns, and pronouns.

Grammar Games & Activities That Boost Writing Skills © 2008 by Immacula A. Rhodes. Scholastic Teaching Resources

Players

2–4

Materials

- What's That Noun? game board
- scorecards
- game cards
- pencils

How to Play

1. Each player writes his or her name on a scorecard.

2. One player shuffles the cards. The player places one card facedown on each box on the game board.

3. To take a turn, Player 1 chooses a card. Player 2 (on the right) picks up the card and reads the word, but not the answer. Player 1 decides what kind of noun the word is: a *common noun, proper noun,* or *pronoun.* He or she responds by using a question, such as "What is a common noun?"

4. Player 2 checks the answer on the card.

   - If the response matches, Player 1 earns the points shown on the box. Player 1 writes the points on his or her scorecard and keeps the card.

   - If incorrect, Player 1 writes 0 on the scorecard. Then he or she puts the card on the bottom of the stack and places a new card facedown on the box.

5. For each player's turn, the player on the right reads the word card and checks the answer. When all the boxes have been uncovered, each player adds his or her score. The player with the highest score wins!

Grammar Guide

A noun names a person, place, thing, or idea. Nouns can be common or proper.
- A common noun names any person, animal, place, thing, or idea.
- A common noun always begins with a lowercase letter.
- A proper noun names a specific person, animal, place, thing, or idea.
- A proper noun always begins with a capital letter.
- A pronoun takes the place of a noun. The most common pronouns are: *I, you, he, she, it, me, him, her, we, they, us,* and *them.*

100	300	500	200
400	200	300	100
300	500	200	400
200	100	400	500
500	400	100	300

What's That Noun?

Name: _____

	Round 1	Round 2
1		
2		
3		
4		
5		
6		
7		
8		
9		
10		
Total		

What's That Noun?

Name: _____

	Round 1	Round 2
1		
2		
3		
4		
5		
6		
7		
8		
9		
10		
Total		

Grammar Games & Activities That Boost Writing Skills © 2008 by Immacula A. Rhodes. Scholastic Teaching Resources

Grammar Games & Activities That Boost Writing Skills © 2008 by Immacula A. Rhodes. Scholastic Teaching Resources

school Answer: What is a common noun?	**police officer** Answer: What is a common noun?	**hill** Answer: What is a common noun?	**Miss America** Answer: What is a proper noun?
state Answer: What is a common noun?	**president** Answer: What is a common noun?	**writer** Answer: What is a common noun?	**New York** Answer: What is a proper noun?
city Answer: What is a common noun?	**lake** Answer: What is a common noun?	**teacher** Answer: What is a common noun?	**Main Street** Answer: What is a proper noun?
girl Answer: What is a common noun?	**month** Answer: What is a common noun?	**computer** Answer: What is a common noun?	**Captain Smith** Answer: What is a proper noun?
road Answer: What is a common noun?	**day** Answer: What is a common noun?	**Dr. Seuss** Answer: What is a proper noun?	**Spiderman** Answer: What is a proper noun?

Hooper High School Answer: What is a proper noun?	**April** Answer: What is a proper noun?	**he** Answer: What is a pronoun?	**her** Answer: What is a pronoun?
Hank Aaron Answer: What is a proper noun?	**Red River** Answer: What is a proper noun?	**she** Answer: What is a pronoun?	**we** Answer: What is a pronoun?
George Washington Answer: What is a proper noun?	**Smoky Mountains** Answer: What is a proper noun?	**it** Answer: What is a pronoun?	**they** Answer: What is a pronoun?
Kansas City Answer: What is a proper noun?	**I** Answer: What is a pronoun?	**me** Answer: What is a pronoun?	**us** Answer: What is a pronoun?
Monday Answer: What is a proper noun?	**you** Answer: What is a pronoun?	**him** Answer: What is a pronoun?	**them** Answer: What is a pronoun?

Grammar Games & Activities That Boost Writing Skills © 2008 by Immacula A. Rhodes. Scholastic Teaching Resources

Planet Plural

Students populate a planet by changing singular nouns to plurals.

Getting Ready

1. Copy the game directions, record sheets, game cards, and answer key. (Enlarge the answer key, if desired.)

2. Color and laminate the record sheets and the game cards. Then cut out the game components.

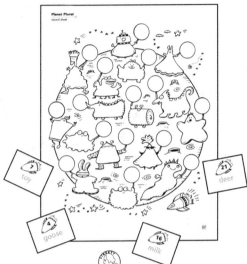

Introducing the Game

1. Review with students the information in the Grammar Guide about changing singular nouns to plurals.

2. Before students play the game, review the game rules and directions with them and model how to play.

> ← EXTENDING THE GAME →

Make a chart that explains the rules for changing singular nouns to plural nouns. Draw a large colored dot next to each rule, using a different color for each. Give students a set of the game cards. Have them decide which rule applies to each singular noun on a spaceship to convert it to a plural, find that rule on the color key, and color the spaceship the corresponding color. After color-coding the spaceships, have children write the plural form of all the nouns on a sheet of paper, grouping the words by color.

SKILL

Regular and Irregular Noun Plurals

Materials

- game directions (page 66)
- Planet Plural record sheet (for each player), page 67
- game cards (page 68)
- answer key (below)
- colored pencils or markers
- scissors
- wipe-off markers
- coin

Planet Plural Answer Key

apple/apples	leaf/leaves
baby/babies	milk/milk
brush/brushes	mouse/mice
calf/calves	pen/pens
church/churches	penny/pennies
cow/cows	shape/shapes
deer/deer	sheep/sheep
dress/dresses	student/students
ear/ears	tooth/teeth
foot/feet	toy/toys
fox/foxes	wolf/wolves
goose/geese	woman/women

Planet Plural

Come up with the correct plural noun for each singular noun on a spaceship.

Players

2 or 3

Materials

- Planet Plural record sheet
- game cards
- wipe-off marker (one per player)
- coin

How to Play

1. Each player takes a Planet Plural record sheet. Players spread the game cards facedown on a table. To take a turn, a player tosses the coin.
   - If it lands heads up, the player takes one card.
   - If it lands tails up, the player takes two cards.

2. For each card chosen, the player reads the singular noun on the spaceship and says the corresponding plural noun. Then the player writes the plural on a space creature on the record sheet and the number of the spaceship on the creature's sign.

3. When all the game cards have been chosen, players check their answers on the answer key.
   - For each correct answer, players keep the spaceship card.
   - For each incorrect answer, players lose the spaceship card.
   - The player with the most cards wins.

Spread game cards facedown.

Record Sheet

Grammar Guide

- Most nouns are made plural by adding -s to the end of the word.
- Nouns ending in *ch, s, sh, x,* and *z* are made plural by adding -es.
- If the noun ends in a consonant followed by -y, drop the -y and add -ies.
- For most nouns that end in -f or -fe, change the f to v and add -es.
- The plural form of some nouns are tricky. For example, the plural of man is *men*.

Grammar Games & Activities That Boost Writing Skills © 2008 by Immacula A. Rhodes. Scholastic Teaching Resources

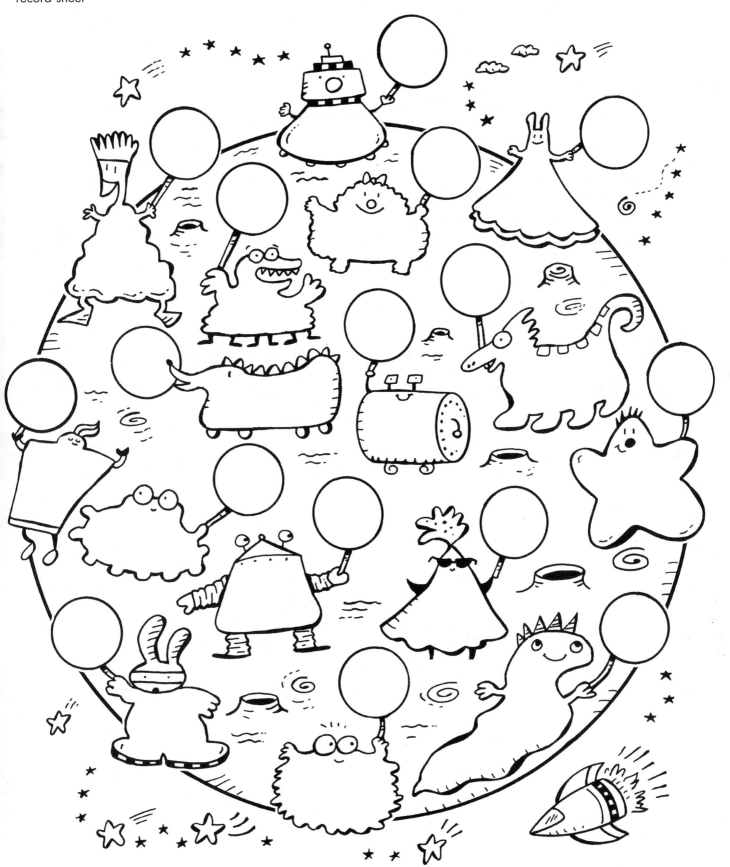

1 foot	2 woman	3 dress	4 goose
5 apple	6 penny	7 toy	8 calf
9 mouse	10 fox	11 leaf	12 pen
13 wolf	14 brush	15 church	16 milk
17 student	18 ear	19 sheep	20 shape
21 deer	22 tooth	23 baby	24 cow

Nifty Noun Magic

Bring irregular noun plurals out of hiding with these rosy sentence pockets.

Getting Ready

1. To make a sentence pocket, tape a long edge of the cellophane one inch over the edge of a sentence strip.

2. Wrap the cellophane snugly around the sentence strip several times, as shown. Staple the cellophane to the sentence strip at both short ends, leaving the long edge of the cellophane open to form a pocket. Trim both ends of the cellophane close to the sentence strip.

3. Add magnetic tape to the back of the pocket.

4. To make magic noun cards, use the black marker to write an irregular noun at the top of an index card. With a red crayon, lightly write the plural form of the noun at the bottom of the card. (To help students learn the singular form of irregular noun plurals, you might also write the plural form of some nouns in black at the top of the card, and their irregular nouns in red at the bottom.)

5. For each magic noun sentence, trim one inch off the end of a sentence strip. Use the black marker to write a sentence containing an irregular noun or its plural form, omitting the noun but leaving a space for it. Underline the space in black, then write "singular" or "plural" under the line. On the line, very lightly write the missing noun with the red crayon.

6. Make a copy of the Grammar Guide for each student.

Wrap around 1½ times. **sentence strip**

10" × 30" cellophane

pocket opening

Staple ends and trim.

SKILL

Irregular Noun Plurals

Materials

- 3- by 24-inch sentence strips
- 10- by 30-inch strip of red cellophane wrap
- tape
- stapler
- magnetic tape
- 3- by 5-inch unlined index cards
- black permanent marker
- red crayon
- magnetic chalkboard (or wipe-off board)
- Grammar Guide (page 70)

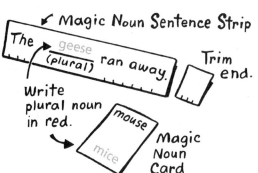

Magic Noun Sentence Strip

The geese (plural) ran away.

Trim end.

Write plural noun in red.

mouse / mice

Magic Noun Card

Introducing the Activity

1. Review with students the information in the Grammar Guide about irregular noun plurals.

2. To use the sentence pocket, attach it to a magnetic chalkboard (or wipe-off board). Insert an irregular-noun card so that the word in red is hiding in the rose-colored pocket. Have students read the word in black. Then ask them to name the plural (or singular) form of the word. To check their work, have students remove the card and read the word in red.

3. For sentences, insert a sentence strip into the pocket. Near the pocket, on chart paper or the chalkboard, write both the singular and plural forms of the hidden noun.

4. On a separate sheet of paper, ask students to write the sentence, and fill in the hidden word. Have them remove the sentence strip to check their work.

EXTENSION ACTIVITY

Invisible Irregular Nouns

Students make irregular nouns instantly appear with these self-checking sentences.

For additional practice, invite students to make up sentence pairs, with one sentence containing an irregular noun and the second its plural form (such as *mouse* and *mice*). After they have their sentences in mind, tell students that they will write the sentences, making the irregular noun an invisible word in each one. Have them use a permanent marker to write the two sentences on a half-sheet of white paper, leaving a space for each irregular noun. Then give them a white crayon to use to write the noun in the space. When finished, ask each student to exchange his or her paper with a classmate. Have students paint a watercolor wash over each sentence. Then ask them to read the sentences, checking for correct use and spelling of the now visible irregular nouns.

Grammar Guide

The plural form of some irregular nouns can be tricky and unpredictable. A few examples of irregular nouns and their plural forms are:

man; men	woman; women	child; children
mouse; mice	goose; geese	tooth; teeth
foot; feet	fish; fish	sheep; sheep

Verb Viper

Students explore the present, past, and future tense of regular verbs.

Getting Ready

1. Copy the game directions, game board, game markers, and the game card pages.

2. Color and laminate the game board, game markers, and the game cards. Then cut out the game components.

3. Fold each game marker so that it stands up.

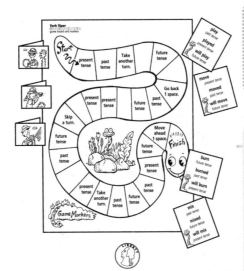

SKILL

Regular Verbs: Present, Past, and Future Tense

Materials

- game directions (page 72)
- game board (page 73)
- game markers (page 73)
- game cards (pages 74–75)
- colored pencils or markers
- scissors
- coin

Introducing the Game

1. Review with students the following information about verbs:

   - A verb is a word that shows action or a state of being.
   - An action verb shows either physical or mental action. It describes what a person, place, or thing does.
   - The tense of a verb tells when the action or state of being takes place.
     - A present tense verb expresses action that is taking place now.
     - A future tense verb expresses action that will take place any time after the present.
     - A past tense verb expresses action that has already taken taken place. To make regular verbs past tense, add -d or -ed.

2. Before students play the game, review the game rules and directions with them and model how to play.

EXTENDING THE GAME

Place the game cards in a paper bag. Tell students to fold a sheet of paper in thirds. Let them pick a card from the bag and read the verbs on it. Have them write a sentence on each section of their paper, using a different tense of the verb in each sentence. Invite students to illustrate their sentences.

Verb Viper

Explore the present, past, and future tense of verbs.

Players
2–3

Materials

- Verb Viper game board
- game markers
- game cards
- coin

How to Play

1. Each player chooses a game marker and stands it on Start.

2. One player shuffles the cards and places the stack facedown.

3. Player 1 tosses the coin.
   - If it lands heads up, the player moves his or her marker one space.
   - If it lands tails up, the player moves two spaces. The player follows the directions on the space.
   - If the player lands on a space marked with "present," "past," or "future," he or she picks the top card from the stack and hands it to Player 2 (on the right). Player 2 reads aloud each verb on the card, but not the small print under the verbs.

4. Player 1 tells which verb matches the same tense named on the space. Player 2 checks the answer.
   - If correct, Player 2 gives the card to Player 1 to keep.
   - If incorrect, Player 2 puts the card on the bottom of the stack.

5. For each player's turn, the player on the right reads the verbs and checks the answer. When all the players reach Finish, they count their cards. The player with the most cards wins!

Shuffle game cards.

Verb Viper

Game marker

Grammar Guide

- A verb is a word that shows action or a state of being. It describes what a person, place, or thing is or does.
- The tense of a verb tells when the action or state of being takes place:
  - A present tense verb expresses action that is taking place now.
  - A future tense verb expresses action that will take place any time after the present.
  - A past tense verb expresses action that has already taken place. To make regular verbs past tense, add -d or -ed.

Grammar Games & Activities That Boost Writing Skills © 2008 by Immacula A. Rhodes. Scholastic Teaching Resources

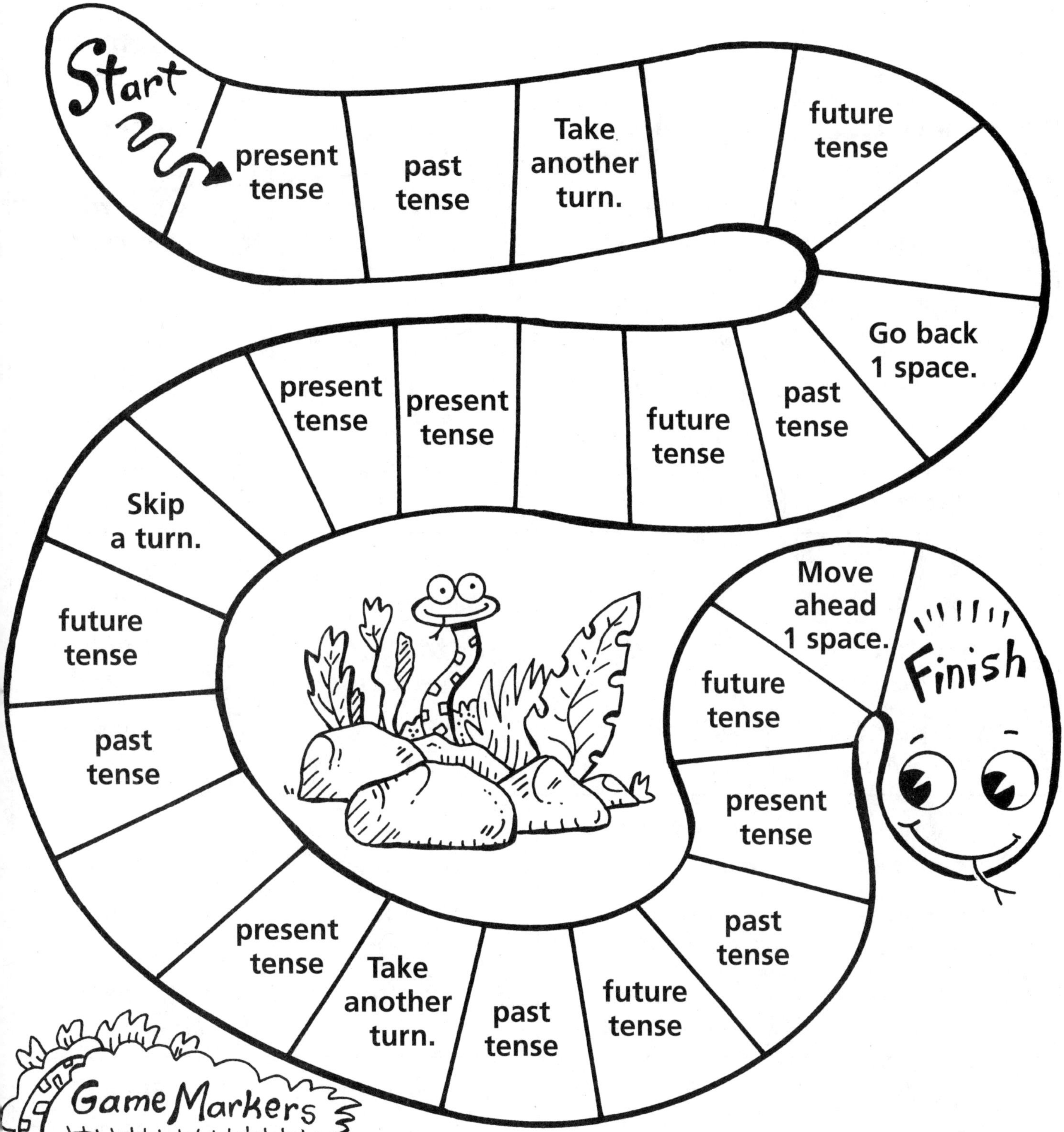

Verb Viper

game board and markers

Start

present tense

past tense

Take another turn.

future tense

Go back 1 space.

present tense

present tense

future tense

past tense

Skip a turn.

future tense

past tense

Move ahead 1 space.

Finish

future tense

present tense

past tense

future tense

present tense

Take another turn.

past tense

future tense

Game Markers

(fold)

(fold)

(fold)

move *present tense* **moved** *past tense* **will move** *future tense*	**roll** *present tense* **rolled** *past tense* **will roll** *future tense*	**step** *present tense* **stepped** *past tense* **will step** *future tense*	**turn** *present tense* **turned** *past tense* **will turn** *future tense*
open *present tense* **opened** *past tense* **will open** *future tense*	**rub** *present tense* **rubbed** *past tense* **will rub** *future tense*	**stir** *present tense* **stirred** *past tense* **will stir** *future tense*	**walk** *present tense* **walked** *past tense* **will walk** *future tense*
paint *present tense* **painted** *past tense* **will paint** *future tense*	**shout** *present tense* **shouted** *past tense* **will shout** *future tense*	**talk** *present tense* **talked** *past tense* **will talk** *future tense*	**wash** *present tense* **washed** *past tense* **will wash** *future tense*
play *present tense* **played** *past tense* **will play** *future tense*	**smell** *present tense* **smelled** *past tense* **will smell** *future tense*	**tap** *present tense* **tapped** *past tense* **will tap** *future tense*	**work** *present tense* **worked** *past tense* **will work** *future tense*
push *present tense* **pushed** *past tense* **will push** *future tense*	**smile** *present tense* **smiled** *past tense* **will smile** *future tense*	**try** *present tense* **tried** *past tense* **will try** *future tense*	**zip** *present tense* **zipped** *past tense* **will zip** *future tense*

ask *present tense* **asked** *past tense* **will ask** *future tense*	**close** *present tense* **closed** *past tense* **will close** *future tense*	**drop** *present tense* **dropped** *past tense* **will drop** *future tense*	**listen** *present tense* **listened** *past tense* **will listen** *future tense*
brush *present tense* **brushed** *past tense* **will brush** *future tense*	**cook** *present tense* **cooked** *past tense* **will cook** *future tense*	**fold** *present tense* **folded** *past tense* **will fold** *future tense*	**look** *present tense* **looked** *past tense* **will look** *future tense*
burn *present tense* **burned** *past tense* **will burn** *future tense*	**crack** *present tense* **cracked** *past tense* **will crack** *future tense*	**jump** *present tense* **jumped** *past tense* **will jump** *future tense*	**march** *present tense* **marched** *past tense* **will wash** *future tense*
clap *present tense* **clapped** *past tense* **will clap** *future tense*	**dance** *present tense* **danced** *past tense* **will dance** *future tense*	**kick** *present tense* **kicked** *past tense* **will kick** *future tense*	**miss** *present tense* **missed** *past tense* **will miss** *future tense*
climb *present tense* **climbed** *past tense* **will climb** *future tense*	**dream** *present tense* **dreamed** *past tense* **will dream** *future tense*	**laugh** *present tense* **laughed** *past tense* **will laugh** *future tense*	**mix** *present tense* **mixed** *past tense* **will mix** *future tense*

Verb Match-Ups

Play this match game with students to reinforce present and past tense forms of irregular verbs.

SKILL

Irregular Verbs:
Present and Past Tense

Materials

- game directions (page 77)
- verb cards (page 78)
- scissors

Verb Pairs

begin/began	keep/kept
blow/blew	leave/left
break/broke	run/ran
buy/bought	say/said
catch/caught	sing/sang
draw/drew	stand/stood
drink/drank	take/took
fly/flew	tell/told
go/went	think/thought
grow/grew	throw/threw
hide/hid	wear/wore
hold/held	write/wrote

Teaching Tip

As an extra challenge for the game, tell players they must also use the future tense of the verb in a sentence.

Getting Ready

1. Copy the game directions and verb cards, laminate for durability. Cut apart the verb cards.

2. If desired, write other verb pairs using the blank cards. See suggestions, left.

Introducing the Game

1. Review with students the information in the Grammar Guide that tells about the present and past tense of irregular verbs.

2. Before students play the game, review the game rules and directions with them and model how to play.

EXTENDING THE GAME

Musical Verb Walk

Reinforce students' knowledge of present and past tense forms of irregular verbs with this stone walk game.

1. Cut out large, irregular-shaped construction-paper stones. Write the present tense of a verb on one side of each stone and its past tense on the other side. Then laminate all the stones.

2. Arrange the stones in a circular path on the floor—with either all the present tense or past tense forms of the verbs faceup.

3. Have students stand on the stones, and then play some music. While the music plays, students walk around the path from stone to stone. When you stop the music, they stop walking and stand on the nearest stone.

4. Students then take turns reading the verbs on their stones, naming the opposite tense for the verbs, and checking their answers by looking at the back of the stone.

Verb Match-Ups

Match the cards to find the present tense verb
that goes with each past tense verb.

How to Play

1. Place the cards facedown on a table.

2. The first player turns over two cards and reads the verbs.

   - If the two verbs make a present-past tense match, the player keeps the cards.
   - If the verbs are not a match, the player returns the cards facedown to the table and play moves to the next player.

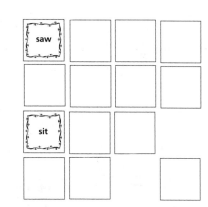

matched
pair →

Players

2

Materials

- game cards

3. Each time a player finds a match, he or she must tell which verb is in the present tense and which is in the past tense. Then the player must use the verbs in sentences.

4. Players continue taking turns until they find all the verb matches.

Grammar Guide

- When an irregular verb forms a past tense, its spelling changes in an unpredictable way.
- The past tense of irregular verbs can look very different from the present tense.
- The past tense of some irregular verbs are spelled and pronounced exactly like the present tense (as with *beat, cut, rid,* and *set*).
- Use the present tense of an irregular verb after *will* to form its future tense form.

sit	see	know	win
sat	saw	knew	won
come	fall	eat	give
came	fell	ate	gave

Grammar Games & Activities That Boost Writing Skills © 2008 by Immacula A. Rhodes. Scholastic Teaching Resources

Verb-fection

Students match the present and past tense of regular and irregular verbs.

Getting Ready

SKILL

Regular and
Irregular Verbs:
Present and Past Tense

1. Copy the game board and game cards for Game Board 1 on one color of paper and those for Game Board 2 on a different color. Also copy the game directions.

2. Laminate the game boards and cards. Then cut out the game components.

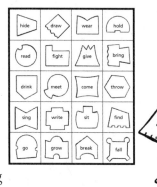

3. Place each set of game cards in a separate sandwich bag labeled with the corresponding game board number.

Place cards in plastic bags.

Game Board 1

Game Board 2

Materials

■ game directions (page 80)
■ game boards (pages 81–82)
■ game cards (pages 83–84)
■ scissors
■ two self-sealing plastic sandwich bags
■ timer

Introducing the Game

1. Review with students the rules about changing regular and irregular verbs to past tense:
   ■ A regular verb can be made past tense by adding -d or -ed to the end of the verb.
   ■ The past tense of irregular verbs can have unpredictable spellings.
   ■ The past tense of some irregular verbs are spelled and pronounced exactly like the present tense (as with *beat, cut, rid,* and *set*).

2. Before students play the game, review the game rules and directions with them, and model how to play.

EXTENDING THE GAME

Give one student a game board and another student the game cards. Have the partners set the timer. To play, the first student reads one verb at a time from the game board. His or her partner finds the matching verb card. Did they beat the timer? Have students switch roles and play again.

Verb-fection

Match the shapes to find the past tense verb
that belongs to each present tense verb.

Grammar Games & Activities That Boost Writing Skills © 2008 by Immacula A. Rhodes. Scholastic Teaching Resources

Players

2

Materials

- Verb-fection
  game boards
- game cards
  (contained in
  2 bags)
- timer

Hint

If the match is
correct, the
shape on the
card will match
the shape on
the game board.

How to Play

1. Each player chooses a
   game board and the
   matching bag of cards.

2. On a signal, one player
   winds up and sets the timer
   for 3 minutes. Then each
   player removes one card at
   a time from his or her bag.

3. Each player reads the past tense verb on the card and
   finds the matching present tense verb on his or her game
   board. The player then places the card on the box with
   the matching word.

4. Play continues until a player matches all of his or her
   cards, or until the timer rings, whichever happens first.

5. When the game ends, players check to make sure their
   verb cards are correctly matched to the words on the
   game board. The player with the most correct matches
   wins the game.

Grammar Guide

- A regular verb can be made past tense by adding *-d* or *-ed* to the end
  of the verb.
- The past tense of irregular verbs can have unpredictable spellings.
- The past tense of some irregular verbs are spelled and pronounced
  exactly like the present tense (as with *beat, cut, rid,* and *set*).

ride	leave	think	do
blow	know	speak	get
sleep	catch	buy	say
eat	see	begin	run
fly	tell	make	stand

Verb-fection
game cards (game board 2)

rode	left	thought	did
blew	knew	spoke	got
slept	caught	bought	said
ate	saw	began	ran
flew	told	made	stood

Verb-fection

"To Be" Cube

Invite students to explore the qualities of the versatile "to be" verbs with this cube.

Getting Ready

1. Copy and color the verb cube pattern and glue it to tagboard. Then cut out the cube pattern and assemble as shown.

2. On chart paper, write six sentences containing the present, past, or future tense of "to be" (both singular and plural forms), omitting "to be" and underlining the space for the word. For example:

   "Tamika [is] eight years old."

   "Yesterday, the squirrels [were] in the park."

   "Next summer, I [will be] going to day camp."

   "I [am] in fourth grade."

   "My aunt and uncle [are] coming over on Saturday."

   "She [was] the first one to arrive."

3. Make a copy of the Grammar Guide for each student.

Glue all flaps.

Fold on dotted lines, with glued flaps on inside.

SKILL

Helping and Linking Verbs

Materials

- verb cube pattern (page 87)
- crayons
- tagboard
- scissors
- glue stick
- chart paper
- markers
- Grammar Guide (page 86)

Introducing the Activity

1. Review with students the information in the Grammar Guide about the verb "to be." Share the examples of sentences to help them understand how "to be" serves as a helping and linking verb.

2. Working with one small group at a time, invite each student to roll the verb cube. Ask him or her to read the word on the top of the cube.

3. Have the student find a sentence on the chart paper in which that verb can be used correctly and then insert the verb in the sentence. If the verb reads correctly, draw a check mark next to that sentence. Then help students determine if the verb is a helping or linking verb.

4. Have each student take a turn as described in steps 2–3, skipping the checked sentences. If the student cannot find an appropriate sentence for the verb, he or she may roll again or make up an appropriate sentence to add to the chart.

5. When all of the sentences have been checked, have students copy them, filling in the correct form of "to be" for each one.

EXTENSION ACTIVITY

Helping Hands

Use these "helping hands" to reinforce recognition of helping verbs in sentences.

1. Tell each student to trace one hand onto construction paper. Have the child cut out the hand shape and glue it to a wide craft stick.

2. Write a sentence containing the verb "to be" on the board. Tell students they will read the sentence to themselves and decide if the verb "to be" is a helping verb. If they determine it is, students hold up their "helping hands."

3. After all students respond, discuss the role of "to be" in the sentence. Write additional sentences on the board, using "to be" as a helping and linking verb.

Grammar Guide

The verb "to be" is used more than any other verb.
- The different tenses of "to be" express a state of being, rather than an action.
  - The present tense of "to be" includes *am, are,* and *is.*
  - The past tense of "to be" includes *was* and *were.*
  - The future tense of "to be" is *will be.*
- The verb "to be" can serve as both a helping and linking verb.
  - A *helping verb* helps the main verb express tense (as in "I am cooking beans" or "I was cooking beans").
  - A *linking verb* shows a state of being. It connects the subject to other words in the sentence (as in "I am hungry" or "You were silly").

glue

glue

glue

am

glue

glue

are

glue

is

was

were

glue

glue

will be

Flip-Flop Agreement Book

Making subjects and verbs agree is a walk on the beach with this unique flip book.

SKILL

Noun-Verb Agreement

Materials

- left and right flip-flop patterns (pages 90–91)
- scissors
- hole punch
- 5- by 10-inch sheet of sandpaper
- 5- by 10-inch sheet of tagboard
- glue
- two paper fasteners
- sticky dots
- Grammar Guide (page 89)

Teaching Tip

To make the activity self-checking, affix the same color sticky dot to the back of each left foot flip-flop labeled with a singular noun and each right foot flip-flop with a singular verb. Then stick a different color dot on the backs of flip-flops with plural nouns and verbs.

Getting Ready

1. Copy and cut out all of the flip-flop patterns. (You may want to copy the patterns on colored paper of your choosing.)

2. Stack all the left flip-flops together and all the right ones together. Punch a hole near the bottom of all the flip-flops.

3. Glue the sandpaper to the tagboard. Punch two holes about two inches apart near the long lower edge of the sandpaper. Use paper fasteners to attach the stack of left flip-flops to the left hole and the right flip-flops to the right hole.

sandpaper

cows   eat

bear   drives

4. Make a copy of the Grammar Guide for each student.

Introducing the Activity

1. Review with students the information in the Grammar Guide about noun-verb agreement.

2. Have students read the noun on a left flip-flop. Then have them flip through the right flip-flops to find a verb that agrees with the noun. When a match is made, ask students to say or write a sentence using the noun-verb combination.

3. Invite students to flip both the left and right flip-flops to find as many noun-verb agreement combinations as possible.

4. To give students additional practice, mask the words on a copy of the flip-flop patterns. Then label the flip-flops with singular and plural nouns and verbs of your choice. Cut out and punch holes in the flip-flops. Replace the original flip-flops with the new ones, then have students repeat the activity to create more noun-verb agreements.

Flip-Flop Relay

Give students more practice with subject-verb agreement using real flip-flops!

1. Bring in several pairs of inexpensive, unused, student-size flip-flops for students to use in a flip-flop relay.

2. To prepare, write a variety of singular and plural nouns on index cards and place them in a basket. Label the basket "Nouns." Then write singular and plural verbs on another set of cards and put these in a basket labeled "Verbs."

3. Place the baskets at one end of the room. To play, divide the class into two teams and station them across the room from the baskets. Then review the following game directions with students:

- The first player on each team places a pair of flip-flops on his or her hands and crawls across the room to the baskets.

- The player then removes cards from each basket, until he or she finds a noun and verb card that agree.

- The player runs the cards back to his or her teammates and reads the noun-verb combination aloud for approval. The first player then passes the flip-flops to the next player on the team.

- When players are unable to make any more noun-verb matches, the game ends. The team with the most correct matches wins the relay.

Grammar Guide

The subject noun and verb in a sentence must agree with each other.

- With the exception of *I* and *you*, if the naming part of a subject is a noun that names one person, place, or thing, the verb ends in *-s* (as in "The dog barks at the car.").

- If the naming part of a subject is a noun that names more than one, the verb does not end in *-s* (as in "The dogs bark at the car").

- You can usually tell if the subject noun and verb agree by listening to the sentence.

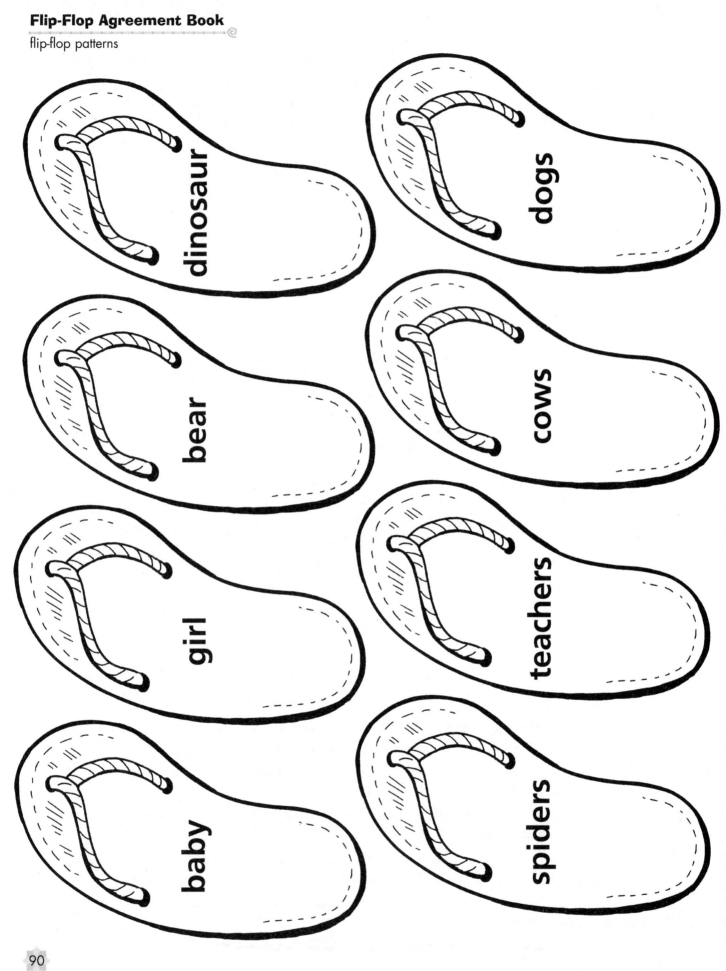

dinosaur

dogs

bear

cows

girl

teachers

baby

spiders

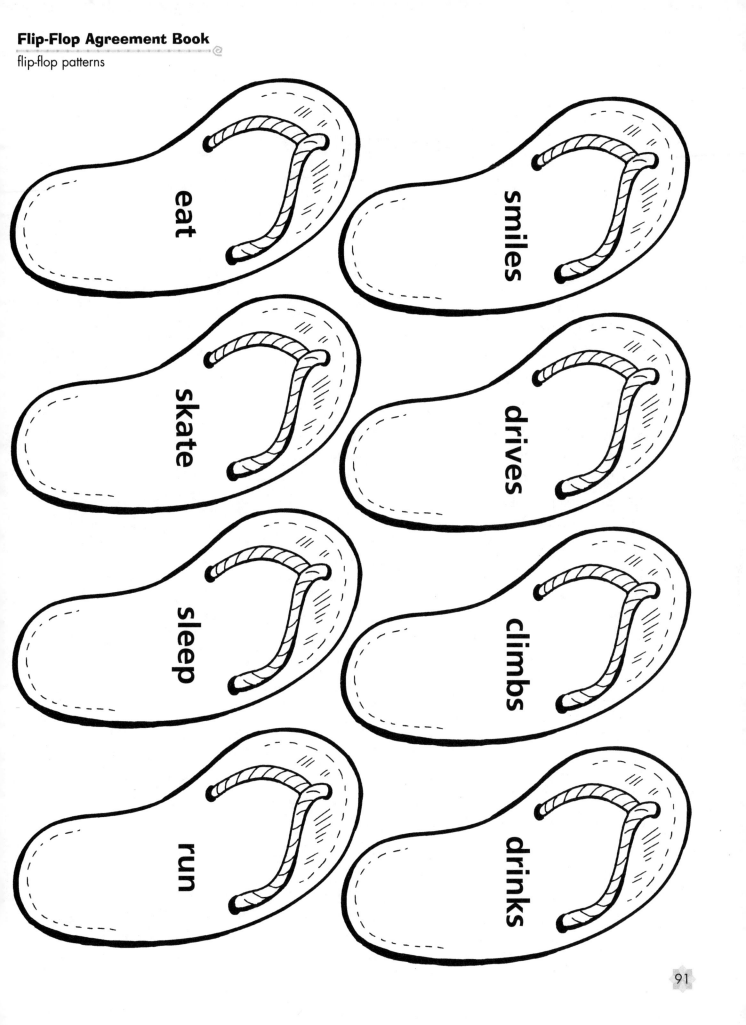

eat

smiles

skate

drives

sleep

climbs

run

drinks

Agreement Gears

Students find verbs that agree with singular and plural nouns.

SKILL

Singular and Plural
Noun-Verb Agreement

Materials

- game directions
  (page 93)
- game board (page 94)
- game cards (pages 95-96)
- colored pencils or markers
- scissors
- paper bag
- game markers (plastic
  counters in different colors)
- coin

Getting Ready

1. Copy the game directions,
   game board, and game
   card pages. (For 3–4
   players, prepare two sets of
   game cards.)

2. Color and laminate the
   game boards and cards.
   Then cut out the game
   components.

3. Put the game cards
   in a paper bag.

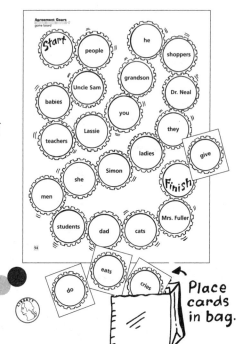

Place cards in bag.

Introducing the Game

1. Review with students the following rules about agreement
   between verbs and singular and plural nouns:

   - If the noun is singular, the verb ends in -s with the
     exception of *I* and *you*.
   - If the noun is plural, the verb does not end in -s.
   - You can usually tell if a noun or pronoun and the verb
     agree by listening to the sentence.

2. Before students play the game, review the game rules and
   directions with them, and model how to play.

EXTENDING THE GAME

Have students write their names on the left side of a sheet of
paper and "I" on the right side. Invite them to pick a card from
the bag, read the verb, decide if it agrees with their name or "I,"
and then write that verb on the corresponding side of their paper.

Agreement Gears

Find verbs that agree with the nouns on the game board.

How to Play

1. Each player chooses a game marker and places it on Start.

2. To take a turn, a player tosses the coin.
   - If it lands heads up, the player moves his or her marker one space.
   - If it lands tails up, the player moves two spaces.

3. The player reads the word on the space. Then he or she takes two verb cards from the bag, reads them, and decides if one of the verbs agrees with the word on the space.
   - If one of the verbs agrees, the player keeps that card and returns the other to the bag.
   - If both verbs agree, the player keeps both cards.
   - If neither verb agrees, the player returns both cards to the bag and the turn ends.

4. Play continues until all the players reach Finish. Then they count their cards. The player with the most cards wins!

Players

2–4

Materials

- Agreement Gears game board
- bag of game cards
- game markers (plastic counters in different colors)
- coin

Hint

Use the words together in a sentence to see if they make sense.

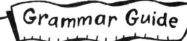

Grammar Guide

The subject noun and the verb in a sentence must agree with each other.
- If the noun is singular, the verb ends in -s, with the exception of *I* and *you*.
- If the noun is plural, the verb does not end in -s.

You can usually tell if a noun or pronoun and the verb agree by listening to the sentence.

Grammar Games & Activities That Boost Writing Skills © 2008 by Immacula A. Rhodes. Scholastic Teaching Resources

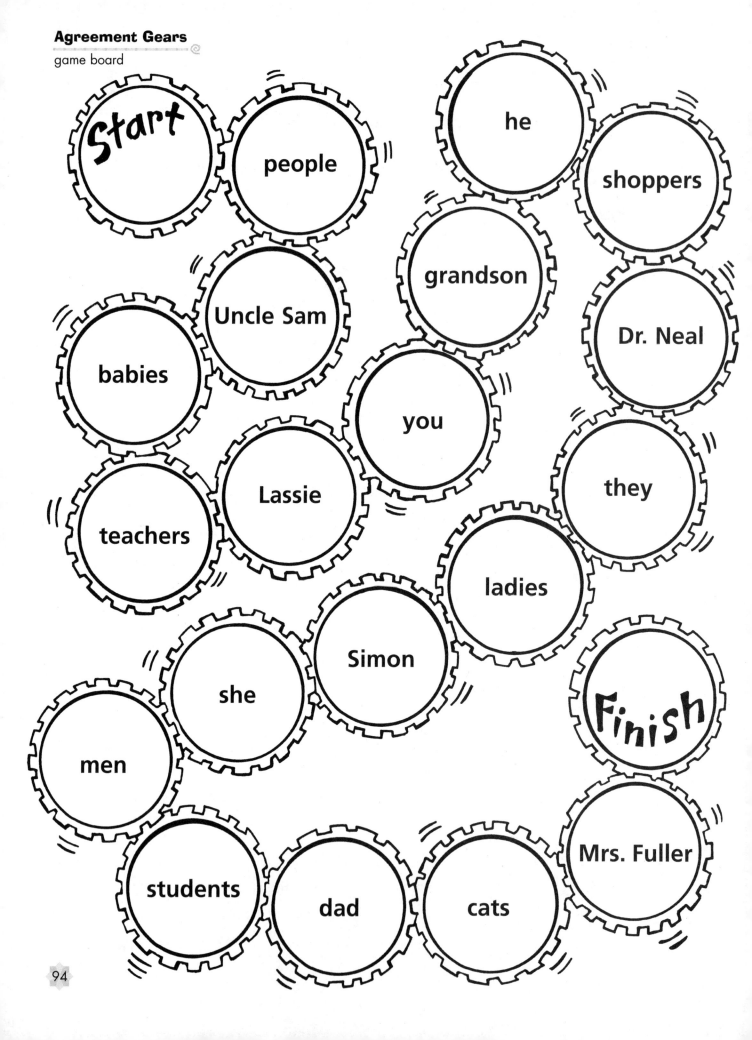

Start

people

he

shoppers

grandson

Uncle Sam

Dr. Neal

babies

you

Lassie

they

teachers

ladies

Simon

she

Finish

men

students

dad

cats

Mrs. Fuller

94

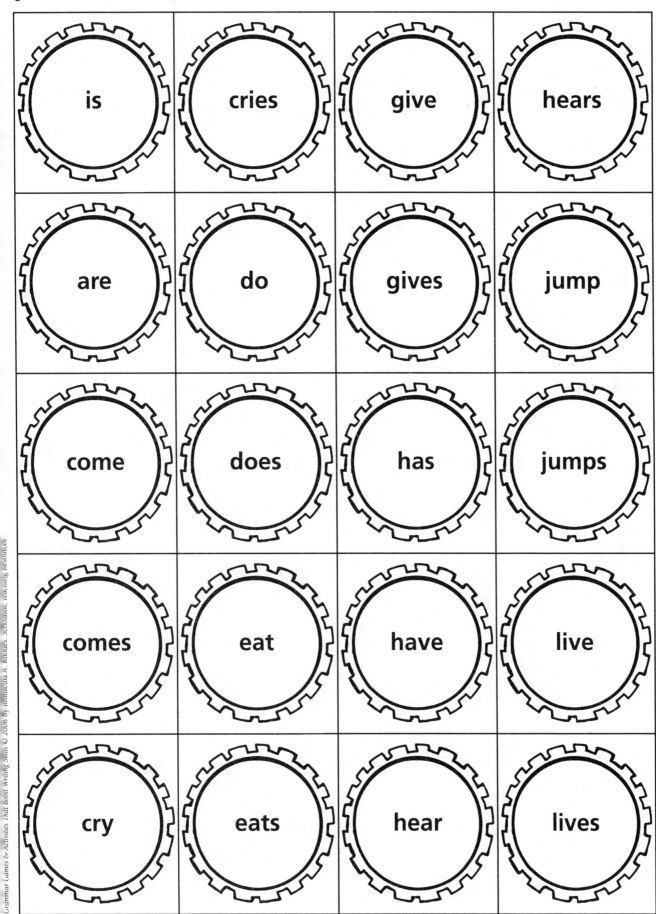

is | cries | give | hears

are | do | gives | jump

come | does | has | jumps

comes | eat | have | live

cry | eats | hear | lives

Grammar Games & Activities That Boost Writing Skills © 2008 by Immacula A. Rhodes, Scholastic Teaching Resources

move	runs	sit	stands
moves	say	sits	stay
ride	says	sleep	stays
rides	see	sleeps	take
run	sees	stand	takes

Grammar Games & Activities That Boost Writing Skills © 2008 by Immacula A. Rhodes. Scholastic Teaching Resources

Giant "I-Glasses"

These giant glasses will help students see how personal pronouns and verbs work together in sentences.

Getting Ready

1. Copy the eyeglass frames pattern, the left and right wheels, and the Grammar Guide for each student.

2. Have students color the the eyeglass frames pattern and glue it to tagboard. Then have them cut out the pattern and the openings where indicated.

3. Show students how to position the eyeglass frame face up and use paper fasteners to attach the pronoun wheel to the back of the lens on the left and the verb wheel to the back of the right lens.

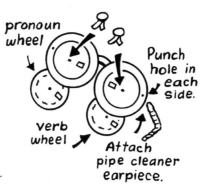

pronoun wheel

Punch hole in each side.

verb wheel

Attach pipe cleaner earpiece.

4. Demonstrate how to punch a hole on each side of the eyeglass frames where indicated. Students then securely attach a pipe cleaner to each hole to serve as earpieces for the eyeglasses. Have them cover the fastener prongs with pieces of sturdy tape.

Introducing the Activity

1. Review with students the rules in the Grammar Guide about pronoun-verb agreement.

2. Direct students to turn the left wheel on their eyeglass frame until a pronoun shows in the opening. Then have them turn the right wheel to find verbs that agree with the pronoun. When an appropriate verb appears in the right opening, students use the pronoun and verb in a sentence to check for proper agreement.

SKILL

Pronoun-Verb Agreement

Materials

- eyeglass and wheel patterns, one each per student (pages 99–100)
- tagboard
- crayons
- glue
- scissors
- two paper fasteners (for each student)
- hole punch
- two pipe cleaners (for each student)
- packaging or duct tape
- Grammar Guide (page 98)

3. After they match all the pronouns and verbs, ask students to turn both wheels so that the openings line up. Have them put on the giant eyeglasses so that they can see through the openings, adjusting the pipe cleaner earpieces to fit their head.

4. Challenge them to search print around the room to find sentences with subject pronouns. When they find a sentence, ask them to name the pronoun and its corresponding verb.

◀ ------------------------- **EXTENSION ACTIVITY** -------------------------▶

Spectacle Sentence-Subject Search

Invite students to use eyeglass props in a special sentence search.

1. In advance, obtain a few pairs of eyeglass frames and remove the lenses. (Use inexpensive sunglasses or shape eyeglass frames out of pipe cleaners.) Put the glasses in your reading center along with strips of paper, pencils, and a list of the subject pronouns. (See the Grammar Guide, below.)

2. Invite student pairs to visit the center, put on the glasses, and then search the reading material for several sentences whose subjects refer to people, animals, or things.

3. When the partners find an appropriate sentence, have one student write the sentence as it appears in print. Ask the other student to write the sentence on another paper strip, substituting a pronoun for the subject (he or she can refer to the list of subject pronouns, if needed).

4. When finished, have the partners remove their glasses, clip their sentences together, and deposit the sentence sets in a basket.

5. Later, separate all the sentence pairs and mix them up in the basket. Whenever a student has a few extra minutes, invite him or her to pick a sentence strip, find the corresponding sentence, and then write the subject of both sentences on a paper strip.

Grammar Guide

When a pronoun is used as the subject, it must agree with the verb in the sentence.

- *I, you, he, she,* and *it* are singular subject pronouns.
- *We, you,* and *they* are plural subject pronouns.

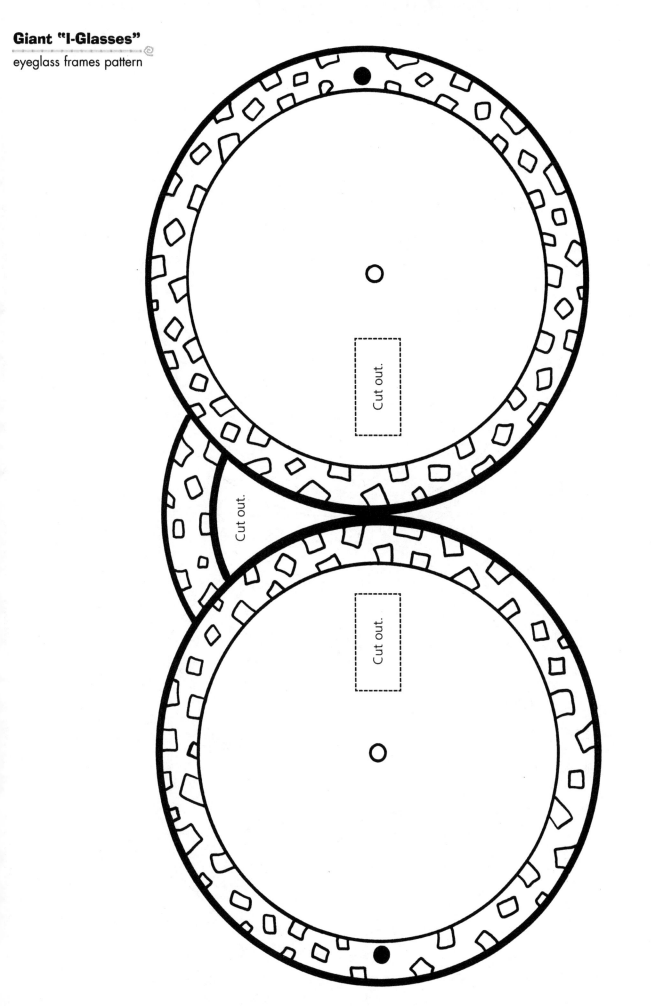

Cut out.

Cut out.

Cut out.

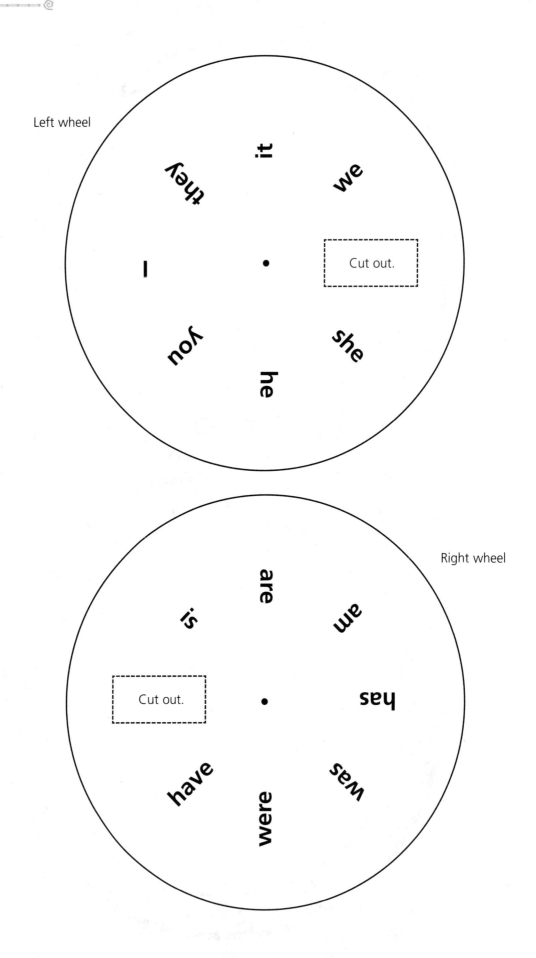

Left wheel

Right wheel

Adjective Hatch

Introduce adjectives by the dozen with these surprise-filled word eggs.

Getting Ready

1. On each slip of paper write a different adjective that can be used to describe an object in the classroom.

2. Fold each paper slip and put it inside a plastic egg. Place the eggs in the egg carton.

3. Make a copy of the Grammar Guide for each student.

Place eggs in carton.

Fold and place each paper in an egg.

soft
blue
shiny

SKILL

Adjectives

Materials

- 12 slips of paper
- markers
- 12 small plastic eggs
- egg carton
- chart paper
- Grammar Guide (page 102)

Introducing the Activity

1. Review with students the information in the Grammar Guide about adjectives.

2. Working with a small group, have students take turns picking eggs from the carton and "hatching" them. Ask students to read the word on the slip of paper. Explain that the word is an adjective—it describes a noun or pronoun.

3. Have students visually search the room to find objects that can be described by their adjectives. Ask them to use the adjectives before the name of the objects being described, such as "yellow flower," "thick book," or "soft bear." Write students' responses on chart paper and have them underline the adjectives.

4. After all of the adjectives have been hatched, ask students to return the slips of paper to the eggs for the next group.

5. If desired, prepare several cartons of adjective eggs. Then conduct the activity using a different carton of eggs with each group, or use all of the cartons to do the activity with the entire class.

EXTENSION ACTIVITY

Adjective Eggs-travaganza

Egg students on to learn more about adjectives with this activity.

1. Give students pairs of large, identical, construction-paper eggs. Direct them to draw a self-portrait on one egg and write words that describe themselves in the self-portrait on the other egg. Have students write their names on the back of both eggs.

2. Display all the eggs with the self-portraits on a bulletin board. Place the eggs labeled with the descriptive adjectives on a table nearby. Invite students to take turns matching the adjective-filled eggs to the ones with self-portraits.

3. When finished, ask students to check the name on the back of each egg in a pair to see if they match.

Grammar Guide

An adjective is a word that describes (tells about) a noun or pronoun.

- Some adjectives describe how many: *few, many, some, ten.*
- Some adjectives describe which one: that, this, those, these.
- Some adjectives describe what kind: *red, big, round, spooky.*

Zany-Zoo Adjective Game

Students find adjectives to describe different zoo animals.

Getting Ready

1. Copy the game directions, the game board, game markers, and game cards.

2. Color and laminate the game board and the game markers. (See Teaching Tip, right.) Then cut out the game components.

3. Fold the game markers so they stand up.

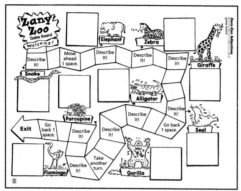

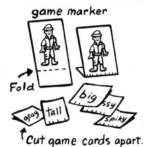

game marker

Fold

Cut game cards apart.

SKILL

Adjectives

Materials

- game directions (page 104)
- game board (page 105)
- game cards (page 106)
- game markers (page 106)
- colored pencils or markers
- scissors
- coin

Introducing the Game

1. Review with students the following information about adjectives:
   - An adjective is a word that describes (tells about) a noun.
   - More than one adjective can be used to describe a noun.
   - Some adjectives describe what kind: *blue, soft, huge*

2. Before students play the game, review the game rules and directions with them, and model how to play.

Teaching Tip

Color at least one animal pink, one gray, and one brown.

EXTENDING THE GAME

Invite students to pick an animal on the game board. Have them find as many adjective cards as possible to describe that animal. Ask them to use the adjectives to write a story about the animal. Then have them illustrate their stories and share their work with the class.

Zany-Zoo Adjectives

Find adjectives to describe the zoo animals.

Grammar Games & Activities That Boost Writing Skills © 2008 by Immacula A. Rhodes. Scholastic Teaching Resources

Players

2–4

Materials

- Zany-Zoo Adjective game board
- game cards
- game markers
- coin

How to Play

1. Each player chooses a game marker and places it on "Welcome!"

2. One player shuffles the cards. Then he or she passes out six cards to each player.

3. To take a turn, a player tosses the coin.

   - If it lands heads up, the player moves his or her marker one space.
   - If it lands tails up, the player moves two spaces.

4. The player follows the directions on the space. If the space is marked *Describe It!*, the player checks his or her cards to see if one of the adjectives can be used to describe the animal in the pen.

   - If so, the player places the card on the box next to the animal's pen.
   - If not, the player keeps all of his or her cards and the turn ends. The player can play only one card each turn.

5. Play continues until one player uses all of his or her cards, or until all the players reach "Exit," whichever happens first. The player with the fewest cards at the end of the game is the winner!

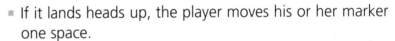

Grammar Guide

- An adjective is a word that describes (tells about) a noun.
- More than one adjective can be used to describe a noun.
- Some adjectives describe what kind: *blue, soft, huge.*

Zany-Zoo Adjectives

game board

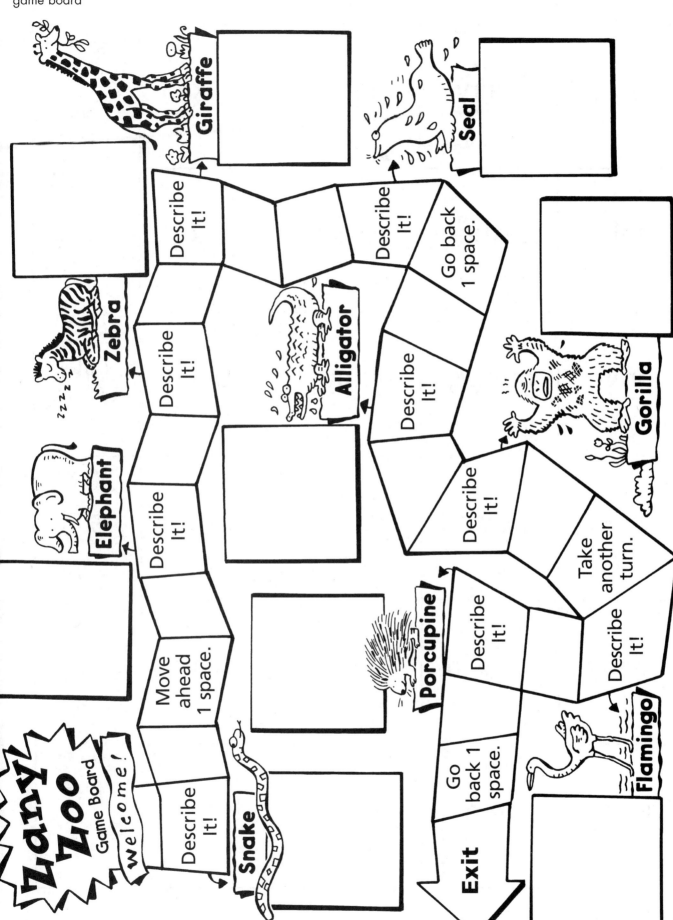

Giraffe

Seal

Describe It!

Describe It!

Go back 1 space.

Zebra

Describe It!

Alligator

Gorilla

Describe It!

Elephant

Describe It!

Describe It!

Take another turn.

Describe It!

Porcupine

Describe It!

Describe It!

Flamingo

Move ahead 1 space.

Zany Zoo Game Board welcome!

Describe It!

Snake

Go back 1 space.

Exit

Grammar Games & Activities That Boost Writing Skills © 2008 by Immacula A. Rhodes. Scholastic Teaching Resources

short	hairy	heavy	spiky
tall	feathery	round	prickly
gray	hungry	bumpy	big
pink	spotted	curvy	little
sleepy	striped	wet	brown
fierce	thin	long	furry

(fold)

(fold)

(fold)

(fold)

Grammar Games & Activities That Boost Writing Skills © 2008 by Immacula A. Rhodes. Scholastic Teaching Resources

Tell-More Toad

This little critter will help reinforce for students what they've been "toad" about adverbs.

Getting Ready

1. Copy, color, and glue the toad pattern to tagboard. Then cut out the pattern and the left and right word wheels. Laminate all the pieces.

2. With the toad pattern face up, use paper fasteners to attach the verb wheel behind the left eye and the adverb wheel behind the right eye.

Attach verb wheel in back.

Adverb wheel is on the right.

3. Make a copy of the Grammar Guide for each student.

SKILL

Adverbs

Materials

- toad and wheel patterns (pages 109–110)
- tagboard
- colored pencils or markers
- glue stick
- scissors
- two paper fasteners
- Grammar Guide (page 108)

Introducing the Activity

1. Review with students the information in the Grammar Guide about adverbs.

2. Invite a student to turn the left wheel to reveal a verb at the notch above the toad's left eye. Then have him or her turn the right wheel to reveal an adverb. Ask the student to read the verb-adverb combination aloud for classmates to perform.

3. To give students additional practice with adverbs, mask the words on a copy of the verb and adverb wheels. Then label the wheels with additional verbs and adverbs of your choice. Cut out the wheels and use them on the toad in place of the original wheels.

4. If desired, invite students to make their own adverb wheels. Then have them turn the wheels to create a variety of verb-adverb combinations. Ask them to say or write a sentence with each combination.

Adverb Hop

This activity will have students hopping for adverbs.

1. Ask students to pretend they are toads. Have them squat down in an open area of the classroom. Then say or read a short sentence that may or may not contain an adverb. Instruct the toads to consider each word carefully to determine whether or not the sentence contains an adverb.

  ■ If they believe the sentence includes an adverb, students give one toad-hop into the air.

  ■ If they do not detect an adverb, they remain still.

2. After students respond, write the sentence on the board. Then ask a student who responded to the sentence with a toad-hop to hop to the board and underline the adverb.

3. Finally, review the sentence word by word to determine whether or not it contains an adverb, and if so, whether or not the underlined word is the adverb.

An adverb is a word that describes or tells more about a verb.

  ■ Some adverbs tell how an action is performed: *fast, easily, hard, quietly*.

  ■ Some adverbs tell when an action is performed: *first, today, now, soon*.

  ■ Some adverbs describe where an action is performed: *here, there, outside, away*. (Some adverbs that tell "where" can also be used as prepositions, for example, *near, up*, and *above*.

■ Many, but not all, adverbs end in *-ly: safely, briefly, gently, yearly*.

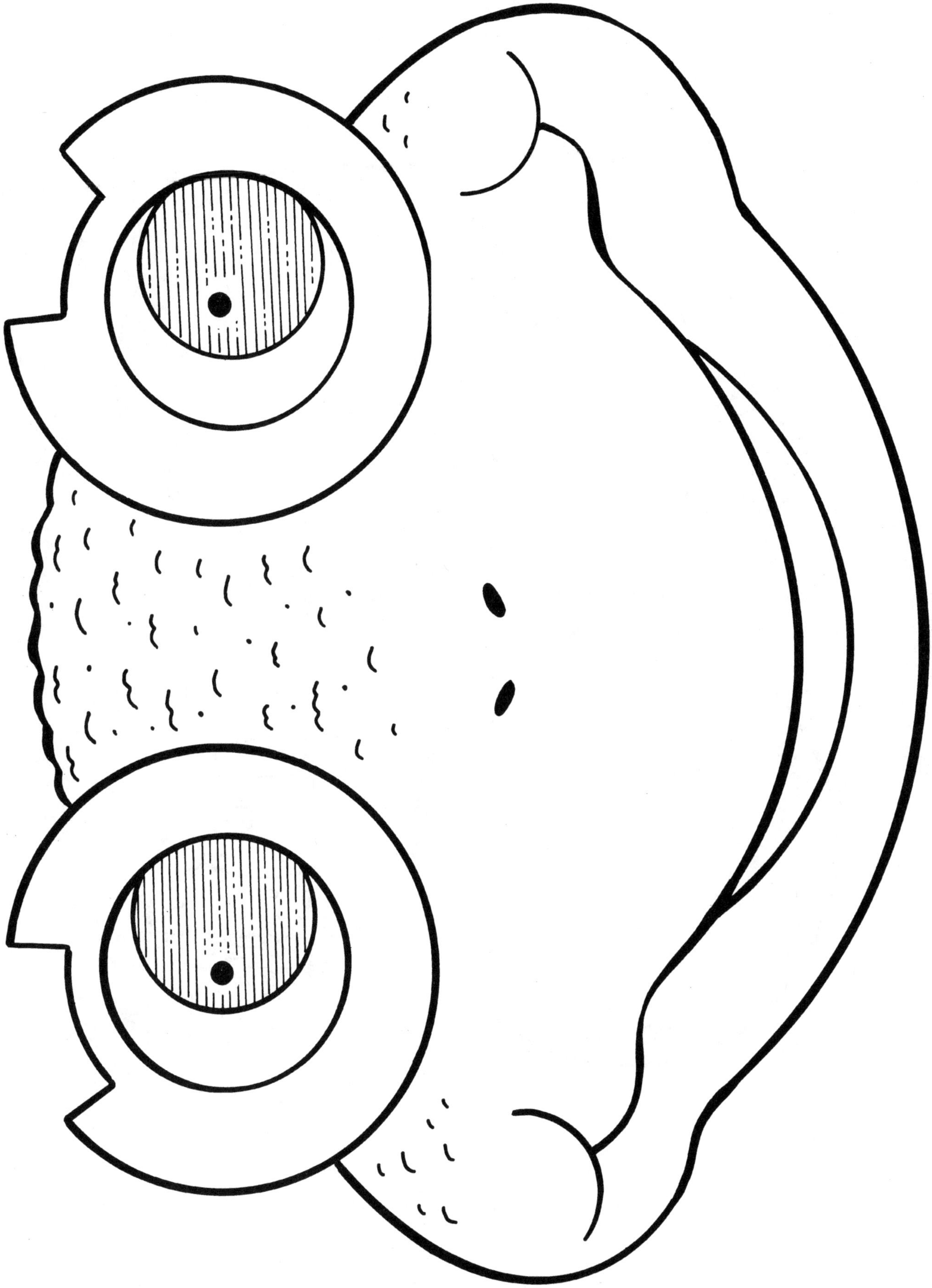

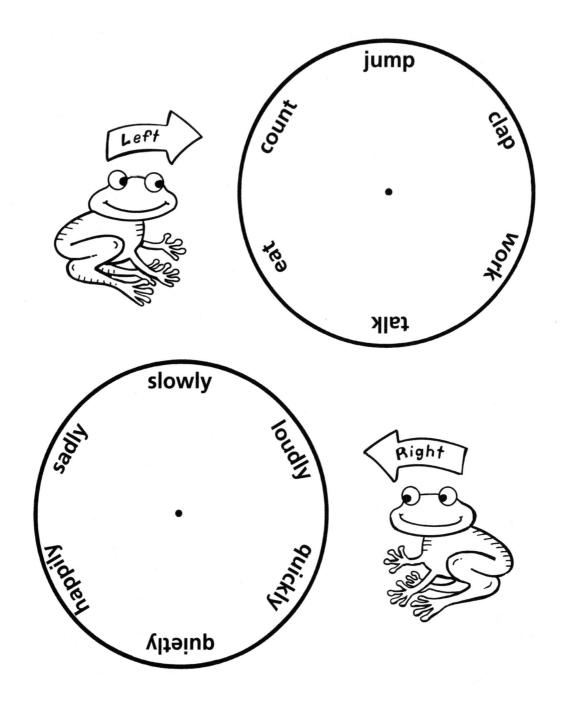

How Now?

Students demonstrate understanding of how adverbs modify verbs.

Getting Ready

1. Copy the game directions, the game board, game markers, and game card pages.

2. Color and laminate the game board, markers, and game cards. Cut out the game components.

3. Fold each game marker so it stands up.

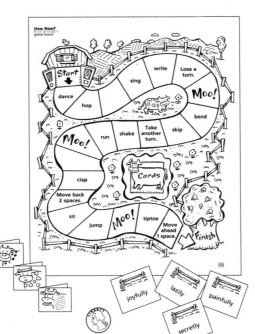

SKILL
Adverbs

Materials

- game directions (page 112)
- game board (page 113)
- game cards (page 114)
- game markers (page 114)
- colored pencils or markers
- scissors
- coin

Introducing the Game

1. Review with students the following rules about adverbs:
   - An adverb is a word that describes or tells more about a verb.
   - Some adverbs tell how an action is performed: *easily, quietly, slowly*.
   - Many, but not all, adverbs end in *-ly*.

2. Before students play the game, review the game rules and directions with them, and model how to play.

◄ EXTENDING THE GAME ►

Place the stack of adverb cards on a table. Then call out an action verb. Invite each student in a small group to pick a card from the stack, read it, and perform the action in the way described by the adverb. Repeat the activity, using a different action verb each time.

How Now?

Pair up adverbs with verbs and perform the actions.

Players

2–3

Materials

- How Now? game board
- game cards
- game markers
- coin

How to Play

1. Each player chooses a game marker and places it on Start.

2. One player shuffles the cards and places them on the game board.

3. To take a turn, the first player tosses the coin.
   - If it lands heads up, the player moves his or her marker one space.
   - If it lands tails up, the player moves two spaces.

4. The player follows the directions on the space. If the space is marked with a verb or *Moo!*, he or she reads the word aloud. The other players then ask, "How now?"

5. To answer the question, the player picks a card from the stack, reads the verb and adverb together, and then performs the action. If the word is *Moo!*, the player says "*Moo!*" in the way described by the adverb. When finished, the player keeps the card.

6. The game continues until a player reaches Finish. If all of the cards are used before the game ends, a player gathers the cards from each player, shuffles them, and places the stack on the game board to be used again. The first player to reach Finish wins!

Grammar Guide

- An adverb is a word that describes or tells more about a verb.
- Some adverbs tell how an action is performed: *easily, quietly, slowly.*
- Many, but not all, adverbs end in *-ly.*

Grammar Games & Activities That Boost Writing Skills © 2008 by Immacula A. Rhodes. Scholastic Teaching Resources

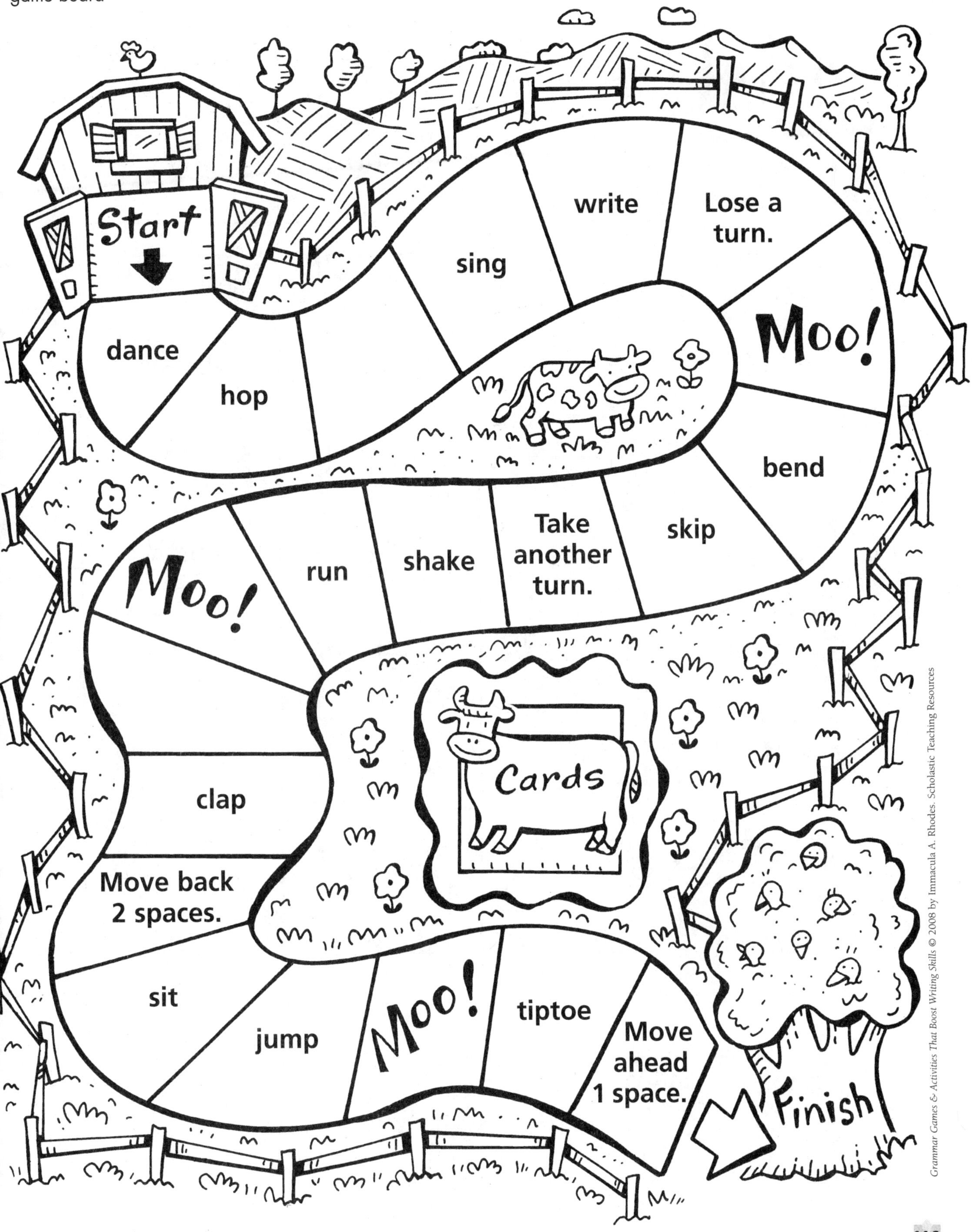

Start

dance

hop

sing

write

Lose a turn.

Moo!

bend

run

shake

Take another turn.

skip

Moo!

clap

Cards

Move back 2 spaces.

sit

jump

Moo!

tiptoe

Move ahead 1 space.

Finish

Grammar Games & Activities That Boost Writing Skills © 2008 by Immacula A. Rhodes. Scholastic Teaching Resources

beautifully	happily	proudly	shyly
carefully	joyfully	quickly	slowly
clumsily	lazily	quietly	softly
excitedly	loudly	sadly	sweetly
gracefully	painfully	secretly	wildly

game markers

(fold)	(fold)	(fold)

Modify Pie

The ingredients in this unusual pie add flavor to even the most plain nouns and verbs.

Getting Ready

1. Copy the pie pattern and word strips. Color the pie pattern.

2. Laminate the pie and word strips, cut them out, and then cut slits along the dashed lines on the pie.

3. To work with adjectives, thread the adjective word strip through the two slits on the left side of the pie. Then thread the noun word strip through the slits on the right.

4. To work with adverbs, thread the verb word strip through the slits on the left side of the pie. Thread the adverb word strip through the slits on the right.

5. Make a copy of the Grammar Guide for each student.

cut slits

Pie Pattern

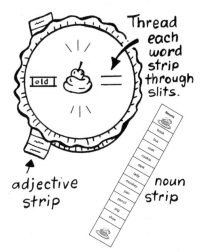

Thread each word strip through slits.

adjective strip

noun strip

SKILL

Adjectives and Adverbs

Materials

- pie and word strip patterns, one each per student (pages 117–118)
- colored pencils or markers
- craft knife (for teacher use only)
- scissors
- Grammar Guide (page 116)

Introducing the Activity

1. Review with students the information in the Grammar Guide about adjectives and adverbs.

2. Invite student pairs to use the manipulative. Instruct them to slide each word strip to show a word on both the left and right sides of the pie, read the two-word combination, and then use it in a sentence. Students can recite their sentences to their partners. Or they can write their sentences on paper for classmates to read and correct, if needed.

3. For more practice with modifiers, mask the words on the word strips and replace them with additional words from the same category (adjectives, nouns, verbs, and adverbs). Thread the new strips through the pie slits. Then have students slide the strips up and down to create more two-word combinations to use in sentences.

4. Invite students to make personal modify pies. Encourage them to use word combinations from their pies to help spark ideas for creative writing topics. Later, have them take the pies home to share with their families.

◄ ---------------------- **EXTENSION ACTIVITY** ---------------------- ►

Hot Potato Modifiers

Naming adjectives and adverbs is a hot topic with this modified game of hot potato.

1. Write a variety of nouns and verbs on index cards. Shuffle the cards and place them facedown in a pie pan.

2. Have students stand in a circle. Explain that they will pass the pie pan around the circle until you sound a signal. On the signal, the student holding the pan removes a card, reads the word, and then calls out an adjective or adverb (depending on whether the word is a noun or verb) to modify the word. Students may not use words already used by previous players.

3. Continue play in this manner until all of the cards have been removed from the pie pan.

Grammar Guide

Adjectives and adverbs are called modifiers because they describe, identify, or limit other words.

- An adjective modifies nouns and pronouns.
- An adverb modifies verbs, adjectives, and other adverbs.

Adjectives	Nouns	Verbs	Adverbs
big	book	begin	fast
cute	bus	come	first
dirty	coat	draw	here
green	cookie	eat	inside
new	desk	go	now
old	lady	leave	outside
one	monkey	read	quietly
short	pan	run	slowly
soft	pencil	speak	soon
that	pig	stand	today
wet	shoe	write	there

Shark Search

Students locate the sharks and identify the part of speech on each one.

Getting Ready

1. Copy the game directions, two game boards, and the game card page.

2. Color and laminate the game boards and cards. Then cut out the game components.

Introducing the Game

1. Review with students the following information about different parts of speech used in the game:
   - A noun names a person, place, or thing.
   - A verb names an action or state of being.
   - An adjective describes a noun.

2. Before students play the game, review the game rules and directions with them, and model how to play.

EXTENDING THE GAME

Have students work in pairs. Ask one student to hide a game board using a file folder screen and then place ten cards on it. Have the student call out the coordinates for the box on which each card is placed and then name the part of speech for the word on the card. The student then challenges his or her partner to place a word for that part of speech on the same box on his or her game board.

SKILL

Parts of Speech

Materials

- game directions (page 120)
- game board (page 121)
- game cards (page 122)
- colored pencils or markers
- scissors
- game markers (large dried beans)
- file folder

Note

Some nouns and verbs in the game, for example, *sand* and *splash* can be used both as nouns and verbs. For the purpose of playing this game, have students use the labels given on the cards.

Shark Search

Find the sharks and tell what part of speech is on each one.

Radar game board

shark cards

file folder screen

Shark Hunter record sheet

Players

2

Materials

- Shark Search game boards
- game cards
- bean markers
- file folder

How to Play

1. One player is the Radar. He or she takes a game board, the game cards, and some beans. The player stands the file folder on the table to use as a screen. Then the player places a card on any six boxes on the game board.

2. The other player is the Shark Hunter. He or she takes some beans and a game board to use as a record sheet.

3. To play, the Shark Hunter tries to find a shark by naming a set of coordinates, such as C3. He or she puts a bean on that box on the record sheet.

4. The Radar checks the game board to see if a shark is on that box. If so, the Radar calls "Shark!" and reads the word on the shark.

5. The Shark Hunter tells what part of speech the word is: noun, verb, or adjective. The Radar checks below the shark for the answer.
   - If correct, he or she calls "Caught!"; removes the card from the game board; and marks that box with a bean.
   - If incorrect, the Radar calls "Miss!"; puts a bean on the box; and moves the card to an empty box.

6. Play continues until the Shark Hunter finds all of the sharks. Then he or she counts the beans on the record sheet to find out how many tries it took to find the sharks.

7. Players switch roles and play again. Then they compare the number of tries each player made to find all the sharks. The player with the fewest attempts wins!

Grammar Guide

- A noun names a person, place, or thing.
- A verb names an action or state of being.
- An adjective describes a noun.

Grammar Games & Activities That Boost Writing Skills © 2008 by Immacula A. Rhodes. Scholastic Teaching Resources

Shark Search
game board

	6	5	4	3	2	1
E	E6	E5	E4	E3	E2	E1
D	D6	D5	D4	D3	D2	D1
C	C6	C5	C4	C3	C2	C1
B	B6	B5	B4	B3	B2	B1
A	A6	A5	A4	A3	A2	A1

small — adjective	wavy — adjective	scary — adjective	pretty — adjective	long — adjective
gray — adjective	sharp — adjective	big — adjective	smooth — adjective	blue — adjective
kick — verb	catch — verb	splash — verb	flip — verb	wiggle — verb
swim — verb	dive — verb	eat — verb	look — verb	throw — verb
ocean — noun	sun — noun	sand — noun	sky — noun	teeth — noun
shark — noun	net — noun	boat — noun	mouth — noun	bird — noun

Pick-Up Sticks

Use this idea to help students understand how parts of speech stick together to make sentences.

Getting Ready

1. Sort the sticks into different color groups. Assign a part of speech to each color. For example, blue might be articles; yellow, nouns; red, verbs; green, adverbs; and natural, adjectives. (If colored sticks are not available, use markers to draw colored dots on both sides of the stick ends.)

2. Use the permanent marker to write a word on each stick that represents the part of speech for that stick color. Use a variety of singular and plural nouns and verbs, as well as past and present tense verbs. Also, you might want to write each of the articles (*a, an,* and *the*) on several sticks. Make sure that each word on a stick works with one or more words on different colored sticks to make a grammatically correct sentence.

3. Put the sticks in the chip canister.

4. Make a copy of the Grammar Guide for each student.

Introducing the Activity

1. Review with students information about the different parts of speech:
   - A noun names a person, place, thing, or idea.
   - A verb names an action or state of being.
   - An adjective describes a noun.
   - An adverb tells how a verb (or action) is performed.
   - An article comes before, or a few words before, a noun. *A, an,* and *the* are articles.
   Then review the information in the Grammar Guide about how the parts of speech are used in sentences.

2. Working with a small group, give one student at a time the canister. Have him or her pour out the sticks and pick one of each color. (Some sticks will land with the word face up and others facedown—the student can pick any stick he or she chooses.)

SKILL

Parts of Speech

Materials

- red, blue, yellow, green, and natural color craft sticks
- fine-tip permanent marker
- short chip canister
- Grammar Guide (page 124)

Teaching Tip

For a game that gives practice using articles, see Articles in the Attic, page 131.

3. Ask the student to read the words on the selected sticks and then put them together to create a sentence. If the word on one of the sticks does not work with the others to make a grammatically correct sentence, have the student exchange that stick for another of the same color. Instruct him or her to make as many exchanges as necessary until a correct sentence can be made.

4. After making a sentence, have the student return all the sticks to the canister and pass it to the next student.

EXTENSION ACTIVITY

Sentence-Construction Concentration

In this small-group game, students concentrate on using different parts of speech to build sentences.

1. Turn all the sticks facedown on a table. Invite the first player to pick one stick of each color. The player then turns the sticks over and arranges the words to form a sentence.

- If a grammatical sentence can be created, the player reads it to the other players, writes it on a sheet of paper, puts those sticks aside, and takes another turn.
- If an appropriate sentence cannot be created with the selected sticks, the player exchanges one stick of his or choice with a stick of the same color from the table.
- If he or she is still unable to create a sentence, the player returns all the sticks to the table and the next player takes a turn.

2. Players continue taking turns until no more complete sentences can be formed. The player with the most complete sentences wins the game.

Grammar Guide

The parts of speech must be put together to express ideas.

- A group of words cannot be a sentence without a verb.
- In addition, a sentence might contain one or more nouns, pronouns, adjectives, and/or adverbs.
- Many sentences also contain articles.
  - An article usually comes just before, or a few words before, a noun.
  - *A, an,* and *the* are articles.

Hands Down!

Students recognize words that are prepositions in this modified War card game.

Getting Ready

1. Copy the game directions. Also copy, color, and cut out the game board and game cards.

2. Fold each game card and glue the insides of the card together. Then laminate the game board and cards.

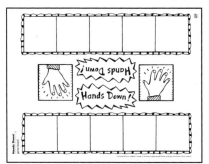 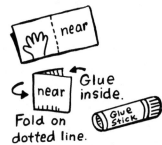

SKILL

Prepositions

Materials

■ game directions (page 126)
■ game board (page 127)
■ game cards (pages 128–130)
■ colored pencils or markers
■ scissors
■ glue stick

Introducing the Game

1. Review with students the information in the Grammar Guide about prepositions.
   - A preposition tells where something is in relation to something else: *on, behind, between.*
   - Usually a preposition found in a sentence is part of a prepositional phrase: *on the table, behind the shelf, between the chairs.*

2. Before students play the game, review the game rules and directions with them, and model how to play.

◄─────── **EXTENDING THE GAME** ───────►

Remove all the preposition cards and put them in a paper bag. Then give students several objects, for example, a book, pencil, and a manipulative, such as a bear counter. Have them take turns drawing a card from the bag. Ask each student to read his or her card and then arrange two or more of the objects to demonstrate understanding of the preposition. For example, the student might put the pencil *inside* the book.

Hands Down!

A preposition wins the round in this dueling card game.

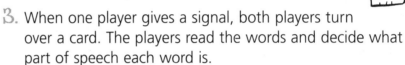

Grammar Games & Activities That Boost Writing Skills © 2008 by Immacula A. Rhodes. Scholastic Teaching Resources

Players

2

Materials

■ Hands Down! game board
■ game cards

How to Play

1. Each player chooses a side of the game board.

2. One player shuffles the cards and places them facedown. Each player takes five cards and places them facedown on his or her side of the game board.

3. When one player gives a signal, both players turn over a card. The players read the words and decide what part of speech each word is.

   ■ If one player has a preposition and the other has a word that is not a preposition, the player with the preposition wins the round and keeps both cards.

   ■ If both cards are prepositions, or neither card is a preposition, the round is a tie. To break the tie, each player turns over another card. The player who wins the tie-breaker keeps all of the cards.

4. Each player places the cards that he or she keeps on a box marked with a hand. Play continues until the first five cards are played. Then each player places five more cards on his or her side of the board to play again. The game ends when all of the cards have been played. The player with the most cards is the winner!

Grammar Guide

■ A preposition tells where something is in relation to something else: *on, behind, between.*

■ Usually a preposition found in a sentence is part of a prepositional phrase: *on the table, behind the shelf, between the chairs.*

Hands Down!

game board

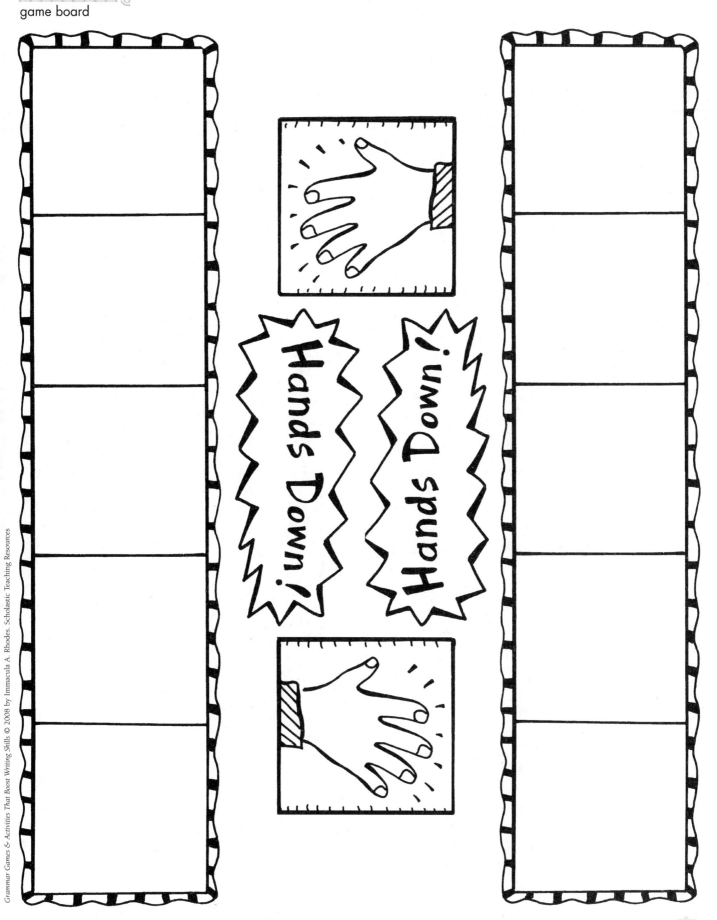

Grammar Games & Activities That Boost Writing Skills © 2008 by Immacula A. Rhodes. Scholastic Teaching Resources

	through		next to
	under		near
	over		down
	above		on
	below		in
	beside		inside

	outside		girl
	off		boy
	around		red
	between		blue
	behind		car
	against		dog

	sad		cat
	happy		mouse
	fast		jump
	slow		sleep
	sit		make
	run		color

Articles in the Attic

Students match a noun to each article in the attic.

Getting Ready

1. Copy the game directions, the game board, and the game card pages.

2. Color and laminate the game board and the game cards. Then cut out the game components.

Introducing the Game

1. Review with students the following rules about nouns and articles:
   - Use *the* in front of a specific noun (*the* book, not just any book).
   - Use *a* before nouns that begin with consonants (*a* cup).
   - Use *an* before nouns that begin with vowels (*an* apple).

2. Before students play the game, review the game rules and directions with them, and model how to play.

SKILL

Articles

Materials

- game directions (page 132)
- game board (page 133)
- game cards (page 134)
- colored pencils or markers
- scissors
- game markers (large, dried beans)
- coin

⟨ EXTENDING THE GAME ⟩

After students play the game, have them remove all the markers from the game board. Ask them to read each article and then name the object that the article is found on (for example, *letter*). Can the noun for the name of the object be used correctly after that particular article? If not, have students name a noun that can be used with that article.

Articles in the Attic

Match a noun to each article in the attic.

Players

2 or 3

Materials

- Articles in the Attic game board
- game cards
- coin
- bean markers

Hint

Once a marker is placed on an article, that article may not be used again.

How to Play

1. One player shuffles the cards and places the stack facedown.

2. To take a turn, a player tosses the coin.
   - If it lands heads up, the player picks one card.
   - If it lands tails up, the player picks two cards.

3. The player reads the noun on each card. Then the player searches the attic to find an article (*a, an,* or *the*) that can be used just before the noun in a sentence.
   - If the player finds a match, he or she places a marker on the article and keeps the card.
   - If the player does not find a match, he or she puts the card on the bottom of the stack.

4. Play continues until all the articles, or as many as possible, are covered. Then each player counts his or her cards. The player with the most cards wins!

Grammar Guide

- Use *the* in front of a specific noun (*the* book, not just any book).
- Use *a* before nouns that begin with consonants (*a* cup).
- Use *an* before nouns that begin with vowels (*an* apple).

Grammar Games & Activities That Boost Writing Skills © 2008 by Immacula A. Rhodes. Scholastic Teaching Resources

Grammar Games & Activities That Boost Writing Skills © 2008 by Immacula A. Rhodes. Scholastic Teaching Resources

ant	gate	mittens	sock
ball	horse	nest	turtle
cars	igloo	owl	uniform
duck	jar	pumpkin	vest
elephant	key	queen	egg
feet	lake	rabbit	worm

Grammar Games & Activities That Boost Writing Skills © 2008 by Immacula A. Rhodes, Scholastic Teaching Resources

Contraction Reaction

Students find the pair of words that make up each contraction.

Getting Ready

1. Copy the game cards and color the bean characters.

2. Laminate and cut out the game cards.

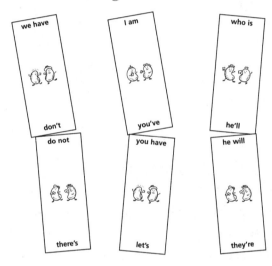

SKILL

Contractions

Materials

- game directions
  (page 136)
- game cards
  (pages 137–139)
- colored pencils or markers
- scissors
- small paper plates
  (one per player)
- game markers
  (large, dried beans)

Introducing the Game

1. Review with students the following information about contractions:
- Contractions are two words that have been squeezed together into one word.
- When a contraction is formed, one or more letters are removed and replaced with an apostrophe.

2. Before students play the game, review the game rules and directions with them, and model how to play.

EXTENDING THE GAME

Pass out all of the cards to students (some may get more than one card). Have one student read the end of his or her card that has the word pair. Ask the student with the corresponding contraction to read that contraction on his or her card. Then have that student read the word pair at the other end of the card. Continue until play circles back to the first student.

Contraction Reaction

Match each contraction to its word pair.

Players

2–3

Materials

- Contraction Reaction game cards
- 2 paper plates
- bean markers

How to Play

1. Each player takes a paper plate.

2. One player shuffles the cards and passes out three cards to each player. The player puts the stack of cards facedown on the table. Then he or she turns over the top card and places it in the center of the playing area.

3. To take a turn, a player checks to see if he or she has a contraction or word pair that matches the card on the table.

   - If so, he or she places the matching end of the card next to that card. Then the player places a bean on his or her plate and picks the top card from the stack. (The player may play only one card per turn.)

   - If a player does not have a match, the player says "Pass," and play moves to the next player.

4. Play continues until as many matches as possible have been made. When the game ends, each player counts his or her beans. The player with the most beans is the winner!

Grammar Guide

- Contractions are two words that have been squeezed together into one word.
- When a contraction is formed, one or more letters are removed and replaced with an apostrophe.

Grammar Games & Activities That Boost Writing Skills © 2008 by Immacula A. Rhodes, Scholastic Teaching Resources

what is	I am	let us	we have
we're	you've	it'll	don't
we are	you have	it will	do not
I'm	let's	we've	there's

Grammar Games & Activities That Boost Writing Skills © 2008 by Immacula A. Rhodes. Scholastic Teaching Resources

there is	I will	it is	that is
we're	wasn't	you're	can't
we are	was not	you are	can not
I'll	it's	that's	I've

Grammar Games & Activities That Boost Writing Skills © 2008 by Immacula A. Rhodes, Scholastic Teaching Resources

I have	he will	here is	will not
who's	they're	we'll	she's
who is	they are	we will	she is
he'll	here's	won't	what's

Grammar Games & Activities That Boost Writing Skills © 2008 by Immacula A. Rhodes. Scholastic Teaching Resources

Katydid, Katydidn't

Students put together verbs and the word *not* to make contractions.

SKILL

Contractions With *Not*

Materials

- game directions (page 141)
- game board (page 142)
- scorecards (page 143)
- game markers (page 143)
- game cards (page 144)
- colored pencils or markers
- scissors
- coin
- pencils

Getting Ready

1. Copy the game directions, the game board, game markers, and game card pages.

2. Color and laminate the game board, markers, and the game cards. Cut out the game components.

3. Fold each game marker so it stands up.

Introducing the Game

1. Review with students the following information about contractions formed from the word *not*:
   - Contractions formed from the word *not* are some of the most common contractions.
   - For most *not* contractions, a verb and *not* are put together, then *o* is removed and replaced with an apostrophe.
   - Exceptions to the above are *can not* (can't) and *will not* (won't).

2. Before students play the game, review the game rules and directions with them, and model how to play.

◄———— EXTENDING THE GAME ————►

Invite students to make up personalized sentences using the contractions written on their scorecards. To do this, have them begin each sentence with their name or *I* and then continue the sentence with the contraction. (This will work with all of the contractions except *aren't* and *weren't*.) Ask students to share their sentences with the class.

Katydid, Katydidn't

Put together verbs and the word *not* to make contractions.

How to Play

1. Each player chooses a game marker and places it on any rock on the game board.

2. One player shuffles the cards and places them facedown on the game board.

Scorecard

3. To take a turn, a player tosses the coin.

   - If it lands heads up, the player moves his or her marker one space and takes the card from the top of the stack.

4. The player reads the card and follows the directions.

   - If the card says "Not," and the player landed on a space with a word, he or she uses the two words to make a contraction. The player writes the contraction and the points on his or her scorecard.

   - If the coin lands tails up, the player moves two spaces and the turn ends.

5. Play continues until all of the cards have been used. When the game ends, each player adds the points on his or her scorecard. The player with the highest score wins!

Players

2–3

Materials

- Katydid, Katydidn't game board
- game markers
- game cards
- scorecards
- coin
- pencils

Grammar Guide

- Contractions formed from the word *not* are some of the most common contractions.
- For most *not* contractions, a verb and *not* are put together, then *o* is removed and replaced with an apostrophe.
- Exceptions to the above are *can not* (can't) and *will not* (won't).

Grammar Games & Activities That Boost Writing Skills © 2008 by Immacula A. Rhodes. Scholastic Teaching Resources

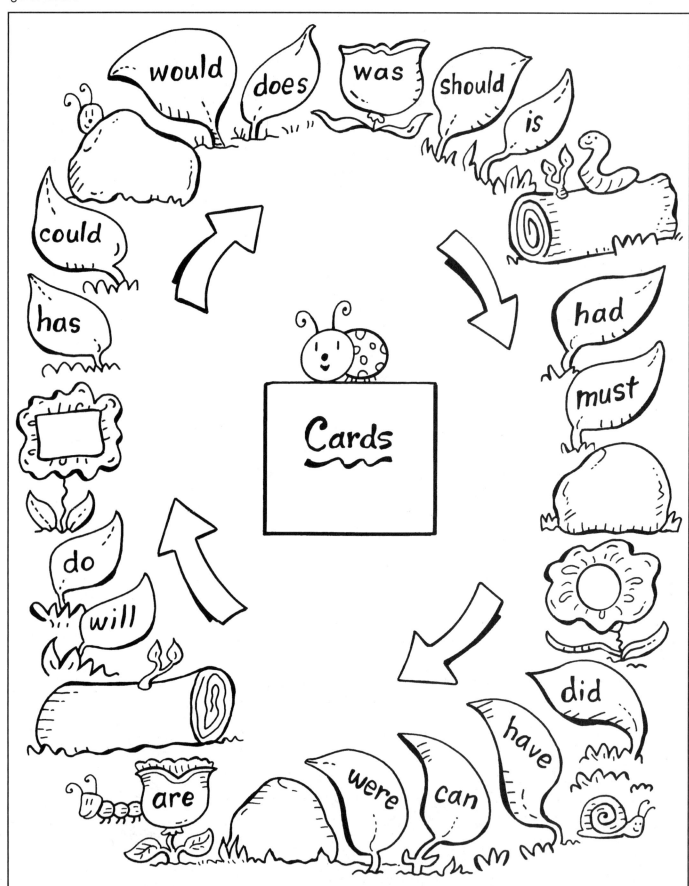

Name: _____

Katydid, Katydidn't

Contraction	Score
1 _____	_____
2 _____	_____
3 _____	_____
4 _____	_____
5 _____	_____
6 _____	_____
7 _____	_____
8 _____	_____
9 _____	_____
10 _____	_____

Total _____

Name: _____

Katydid, Katydidn't

Contraction	Score
1 _____	_____
2 _____	_____
3 _____	_____
4 _____	_____
5 _____	_____
6 _____	_____
7 _____	_____
8 _____	_____
9 _____	_____
10 _____	_____

Total _____

(fold)

(fold)

(fold)

Not 1 point	**Not** 2 points	**Not** 3 points	Take another turn.
Not 1 point	**Not** 2 points	**Not** 3 points	Take another turn.
Not 1 point	**Not** 2 points	**Not** 3 points	Move ahead **1 space.**
Not 1 point	**Not** 2 points	**Not** 3 points	Move ahead **1 space.**
Not 1 point	**Not** 2 points	Go back 1 space.	Lose a turn.
Not 1 point	**Not** 2 points	Go back 1 space.	**Pick another card.**

Grammar Games & Activities That Boost Writing Skills © 2008 by Immacula A. Rhodes, Scholastic Teaching Resources